Offertories:

Exclamations and Disequilibriums

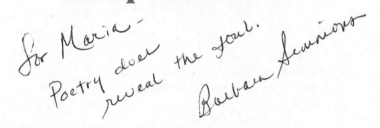

For Maria —
Poetry does reveal the soul.

Barbara Simmons

Barbara Simmons

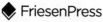 FriesenPress

One Printers Way
Altona, MB R0G 0B0
Canada

www.friesenpress.com

ISBN
978-1-03-913498-0 (Hardcover)
978-1-03-913497-3 (Paperback)
978-1-03-913499-7 (eBook)

1. POETRY, AMERICAN

Distributed to the trade by The Ingram Book Company

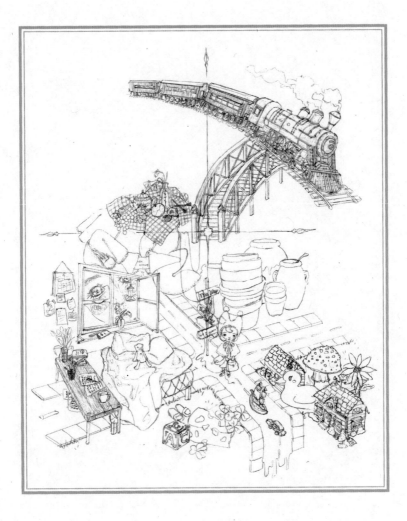

Table of Contents

What's going to happen to my poetry and journals?

This begs the question of what constitutes MY journals. What will happen to all the poetry I've written? My journals are not the neat, well-calligraphed pages of daily musings. Mine are the small post-its, the scribbled notes on the backs of receipts, the singular word that cries on the edges of newspapers, the phrase on the inside covers of books, the 'bon mots' on the margins of a re-read page, the remembered phrases of a poem by Elizabeth Bishop about the "art of losing." I imagine my musings to find their way to my readers—my family, mostly—after I have touched them for the last time, so that my verbal rejoicings and sorrows, my curious wonderings and whimperings, can open me up more fully to those whom I have loved well, but, at times, have not been able to 'erupt spontaneously' to. Just writing an answer to this question as part of a preface to this volume of collected poetry (much coming from what I'd begun to think of in my journals) has required me to imagine all the shelves and drawers, and handbags and boxes, and book stacks and files, and nightstands and table corners, that have held both my impromptu and planned journal entries. And now, this musing helps me display how I discover myself through my reveries, more unedited and unfiltered than any 'finished' work —although what you will be reading has been polished (a bit)—probably closer to the truth that I coax, always, to life.

Thanks to all the journal entries for holding my words in all their raw and wild and abbreviated and cryptic states. And, thank you, readers, for taking the time to glance at what has become of them!

Early Writing Years

*Waltham High School, where I grew up,
and Wellesley College, where I wandered for four years,
learning to love more dearly the sounds and soul of literature*

Bridges to Destiny

Those daring forged
A new path
Through wild and wonderful
Verdant foliage;
Through deep and dank
Textured forests;
Through sand-filled and savage
Desert expanses.
Those adventurous did build
A bridge of oak *and* faith
Among brothers striving
For that cause of freedom,
For the genesis of America.

Those ingenious covered
This bridge that spanned
Cities of Revere and the lanterns;
Cities of Jefferson and the Declaration;
Cities of Hancock and the Constitution;
Cities of power, growing and grasping
New industries of asphalt
Billowing puffs of the black smoke of
Energy. Those ingenious
Poured this liquid cover of
Protection over the bridge.
This bridge paved with power
Endured.
Those discovering will erect
A bridge of tomorrow:
Fibers of invention riveted

To filaments of improvement,
A chain of silver-wired webs
Connecting the present to the
Future.
This bridge will connect the races
Of mankind with a new bond
Of understanding: this bridge will
Cement the peoples of the world
Into one glorious harmony of
Tomorrow.
We are those who
Stand now on a bridge
Of the mind and soul.
Let us be the steel cables
Crossing stretches of time,
Miracles of art and learning.
Let us be the dauntless concrete
Bridging streams of prejudice, rivers of
Hatred, oceans of war.
Let us be tentacles joining the
Blood of patriots to our quest
For freedom, for America, for tomorrow.

Waltham High School, Waltham, MA Class Poem 1965

Cartesian

M. Descartes and his lines,
Appelés le *x* and le *y*,
Pale green graph,
Spun with squares.
And they say
"Life is just a crossroads,"
    a paradise cloven with inferno.

allez.
            point, one-tenth from origin and
            birth.
            negative, turn left, find death.
            womb hollows its placental niche,
                    and Atreus' "seeds of destruction" sprout.

ité.
            dot, two-tenths from source and
            games.
            R.L.S. and a child's garden, up in a swing,
            jump rope, turn and step on your shadow
                    and cross the limits of essence.

va.
            la pointe, over one, up two from nothing and
            cocks.
            red farmhouse, red barn, red hay.
            ruff shredded, turn to sullied soil,
                    and relive "bloody Kansas."

venez.

(0,10). Red Queen to Alice in
Wonderland.
Hurry, hurry. Run come run go.
pinafore starched, chess set
        to play a social game.

come.
        (0,0). Picasso to his Harlequin

dying.
Diamond patches, let color be sucked.
Blues, pinks, bare yourselves for canvas, let
        scratchy hemp rub your soul.

O, Lao-Tse,
        look at this graph,
        this damned and heavenly
        pattern.
        you said the wise man
        can see the small and large,
        knows no ends.
        is there a
        stop
        in my source
        at (0,0)?

Wellesley College Freshman Poetry Prize, Spring 1966

Storm's Over

When the storm had fulfilled
its claims to epithets
bestowed by Homer and weathermen,
we, bundled in windbreakers,
were allowed
by measure of parental authority
to explore an aftermath
of hailstones and torrent.

We would scramble
to the edge of infinity
and penetrate the pretending sea
with knowing eyes
that pierced the guise of
calm, and touched the
tremors of its bristly crests.

Then we'd think of
all the drops that, having
foamed and soaked into
the sand beneath our
shoes, had felt the shores
of other lands, but
now were captives
much like us.

And though you and the sea
remained as loyal as
the moon is the Earth,
or mother is to us,

my fingers hurt, and
grasped at the gusts of air,
wanting to sift sands

as if my life depended on it
and finding only water-
packed grains and
nature's evanescent
immutability.

The Washington and Jefferson Literary Journal, 1966,
The Thoreau Edition

Pastiche

Blue calluses my hands
numbing members of feel
to sharply even bristles,
dried and dead.
a cubist's brush paints me
part fish, sharply woman
in a sea of smiling
toothless dragons.
Curving, my contents
cross a bass, and
cubes of violins try
la lala lalala, my
sonata to myself.
Janus-headed.
Blue patches on
my woman face, a
palette drowns the fish.
Beasts feed on blue,
now our jaws devour all
but shadow.
Flat panels splice the
singular-isms, doer and
done, creation of one,
on a triptych.

Spring 1967, Wellesley College. Printed in Quince, Vol. 1, No. 2, 1968

Eye

Although I, unlike the
sainted maiden whose visions
stepped on magic circles
ringed eternally with light,
have not eyes
to approach golden apples,
holy grails, indeed too frail
for destruction's plucking,
I, with sight
between the lashes of my
eyes, see more clearly than
any stone-frozen head, see
more than those fated
ever to eye their heels,
indeed, do see, will see
shades of blankness, and
striated clarities,
rippled water, which I,
in time, perceive,
perceived, to hold as
much as endless
hands, a sight without visions.

Spring 1968, Wellesley College

From an autopsy report, summer: 1968

*"The usual Y-shaped incision is made
to open the body cavities."*
What procreation does this knife produce,
upon this womb that disavows its fruit
and claims its child
in orphaned words, typology's black
bastards?

Against white sheets, this body and these words
impress barren signs.
A tool now plunders what
once was,
before the metal probe,
inside the lifeless shape,
where words alive once formed
the script that now awaits
the critic's words.

An *"unremarkable throughout,"* this corpse
displays herself in words
atonal and not hers;
the chisel now describes the stone:

she claims gray children.

Waltham Hospital, Summer 1968

Procrustean

each time
a brave new world
pops up
in bands of prophecies
or heresies
I picture a long-haired
Goldilocks in a
papa- or mama-
sized bed
eating from a
papa- or mama-
sized ladle in a
papa- or mama-
sized bowl.
and like the inquisitive miss,
whose needs
demanded
a smaller bed,
I see my
head or
my feet
lopped off
so Sir Procrustes
can enlist
another porridge-eater.

and I know that
minus what
the trees call fingers
I still
will
find my my-sized bed
and eat my
seasons of
suns and moons.

Wellesley College, 1968-69

Johns Hopkins University, The Writing Seminars

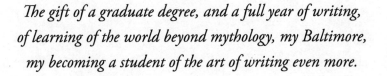

The gift of a graduate degree, and a full year of writing,
of learning of the world beyond mythology, my Baltimore,
my becoming a student of the art of writing even more.

from the horse's mouth

No whip is near
nor needed, though your mouth
cuts both its corners with
a bit. A bit? you mimic
sound, you silent
groveler impossibly inhaling air,
so stop. No bit impedes the shape
that once you groaned
that once you gabbled
gabbed
then drew. You'd spinning
pencil walls, your nostrils
wide, the boy and bull would
time their jumps as if the
legend left its Cretan base.

bullboybullboy jump and
repeat.

With mural dizziness you
run, trained tail-catcher,
biting pictured sounds
around
those walls.
Rear you may, to spit or
vomit out the bit.
I see no bit,
but you, who promised notes
to flute and lyre,

must slowly solve, a Theseus
without his maid, and then
dissolve
the problem twined
about your tongue.

Johns Hopkins, Fall 1969

A Goddess Grown

with thanks to Robert Graves, *The Greek Myths*

Crone,
you flatten me with echoes of
prolonged monosyllabic weight, your hardened
length becomes my frame too well,
becomes and is the pressure on my nose:
you sound my soul with nasal
plumblines.
              I had believed too long
in other sounds, had pumped for youth
when mouths were closed.
                 I was
a goddess then, but then becomes another
sound, and sudden, shrouds the *is* of *now*.
I think
I was those words, at least
a nymph, nubile, young
pupa.
       he showered fertile rain
       upon her secret clefts,
       and she bore grass, flowers,
       and trees.
in silence he had come to me
to plumb the darkness of my youth.

                              I no
longer lie, I know the form the sounding
shapes, and so, a crone caws, caws and calls,
am I a crow? black with no sleek
slope, slipping to this word,
old crow crowned crone,
old me?

Johns Hopkins, 1969

Train: Baltimore to Boston, 1969

I
Before the body moves
it thinks its motion through,
thorough, the thought impels
connections:
tiny racing jumps that hesitate only
to return in sequence
to another point.

II
Alone no motion
can suffice
to separate
the dark-toned room I live in:
> dark amplified by
> pigeons sounding,
> searching for
> new eaves
> and maple trees
> abundant with sweet sap
> encasing branch and branch
> with shaded thicknesses.
alone seeks its relief
with low-pitched pigeons
synchronizing with the train,
hoping that
sound imagined
replaces
space.
Yet alone.

Replacement equals
withdrawal.
silent sound
negative space.

III
       Sartre's mind:
that: people of a same period and
collectivity, who have lived through the
same events, who have raised or avoided
the same questions, have the same taste
in their mouth: they have the same complicity,
and there are the same corpses among them.

so
I claim this train,
its passengers
my compeers. Those hurrying
their lives/along two lines.
complicity containing the fore-
of complications.
I lend myself to compeer-
complicities.
just breathing
sitting here.
We have run,
passengers in a persistent pattern.
We do run.

IV
Escape.
The Latin of a word
defines its soul. The black
strokes define body.
Always two. Too even, this
divided world. Too
many choices.

ex. cappa.

Shed, like the Herculean
garb, the anterior
part of my escape, *cappa,*
lies groaning in a wrinkled
mouth.

V
Axiom. All journeys between two points
            imply a changing from none.
My proof is this train:
encased escape of no escape.
pedestrian: the body and the thought.
iron traceries withhold release.
my body dies beyond the tangent.

VI
The window melts beside me.
Sun with Helios' force
reduces glass,
always toward the myth,
toward spare terms
spare script.

VII
Stare at connected scenes
Through connected frames.
A windowed eye.
The desire for delirium
dizzying.
And still, pedantic, I find
calenture.

> *OED: a burning fever incident*
> *to sailors within the tropics*
> *characterized by delirium in*
> *which the patient, it is said,*
> *fancies the sea to be green fields,*
> *and desires to leap into it*

inviting/
dread.

VIII
The speed I learned
later
was from without.
I cannot run
an enclosed race.
Escapement still controls
the clock, releasing sound
to space on time.
I task myself with worlds of time.

IX
Crocier, crossier. Old
French syllables slide,
while weighted by the staff
I bear, my body moving forward,
I whisper darkness
and begin
      in
      images.

Johns Hopkins, Spring 1970

Duration: Train

There no knowing is
not. Motion: jolting morning
from me. Motion: meaning
moving spaces. My body moves.

It inert
sits
and knows the body of the train
in sectioned space.

Stilled time
exudes
the smells of bodies
still.

          The woman near me reads
the paper like a
homing pigeon, flying to
obits: abbreviation for the
word abbreviates the space
of print, and
of the life.

'Husband's dead ten years:'
sectioned
shreds of life,
railroad widows
measure time in pass-
es. Measure time
through passing
train windows.

             The train is
cheaper for a
railroad widow.

Duration is a hardening.
The smell of time still
with me, the smell of age afraid
of time.
All this endured
for passing
on a
half-priced pass: Good
This Time
Only.

Johns Hopkins, Spring 1970

Return: To Baltimore

I read
where whales
returned to shore to die
when given
back their seas.
Perhaps the shore became
the sea.
>   Whose definition
>   do we mouth
when whales have died for one?

I come back to my shore:
redefined.

How often sounds
have sectioned words
to mean
the sounds.

>   I have divided
you: your sound has come
in darkness til
its whisper
meant all.

So still
I cannot hear
except the pigeons caught
in sap-drenched leaves.
outside this dark
dark room.

O lizard prince,
your sectioned
head
and limbs
and the caboose
that carries
ends.

The choice
of two. I turn
you then
from word to word.

So Grecian prince:
now basilisk.

Define me
with your stare.

Johns Hopkins, Spring 1970

-petal: seeking

Today I would have my head
disappear among flowers, or
bloom.

petal me in winding
sheets, softly.

Like an Odilon Redon
my head in corners floats
detached.

petalled.
me in petals.
soft: the inside:
cat's ears.

watery. my head floats.
decapitated senselessly.

I surround the stigma,
so many petals
round me, winding
centers. Blinding.

Membranes on a fish's eye
I could envy. Seeming
insensate they, glazed, stare.
one eye. one side.
they see both sides, they
can't see one.

petals.
softly wound
blindly shroud.
staring drowned.

hacked.
hand to head: fishman, artist,
sever
me.

                                  fish eyes.
                                  each side.
                                  no eyes. petalled.

One time, when we were not
Blind to each other's side, we
softly saved petals
to dry.

                                  dry the petals.
                                  dry the eye.
                                  blindly shrouded.
                                  wounded dies
                                  soft sight.

head
crowned and dried.
petals wound around my
eye.

Johns Hopkins, Spring 1970

A darkness shining in brightness
which brightness could not
comprehend. ~ Ulysses

Before I believed
I supposed
in contrasts:
>   Dark whisperings
>   against the spoken.
>
>   The habit of returning,
>   remembering
>   intruding,
>   always an entrance,
>   locating people for
>   a past.
>   Then forgetting,
>   surviving the disjunction.
>   surviving for it
>   because of it.
>   then and now.

Radial.
The mythic strands
pull me
to centers
met in one belief.

I counted caves
as centers for the shades
>   of dreams
>   and sight,

supposed them
spokes
for one belief.

The brightness of belief,
a hungry sun,
            a shriveled seer,
tents my caves.

Shades disappear.
            Light is not all.

The shadowed world
alternations.
            Blurred the sun
            Blessed my sight.

Darkness of my bright
beliefs, supposings saved
my sight.

Johns Hopkins, 1970

A Fine Film ~ Roethke

Dust,
I have discovered,
practices fenestration
on walls.

Space proves provender
for dust
where it may reform
edges so
the masculinity of shape
acquires counterparts
in shadow.

Dust,
I have decided,
does not penetrate.
It is, like the world,
too much with us
for relegation to
an act.
Dust: *sine fine.*

Its definition
needs origins.
dust's creation,
the first act. Original.
And now the definition
retells the act until
they are each other.

We are dust.

Dust precludes distinctions.
Shapes sift
as if
to settle into bas-relief.
One bequeaths
one's shape
to twilight.
                        We are dust
                        and shadow.

The hour
defines the dust.
An interval
belies the motion of
a shadow.
        As Chartres
confined light, so we
do dark.
        Til dusk
                        and dust.

Johns Hopkins, Spring 1970

The Twenty-Second

Does no more betray me
than does the staring
into empty glasses, filling
them with wine
deceptive as my gazing.

Diverting the decanter
from the glass, anticipating
the disaster of the drinking
of dreams that are not there,
I deny our silence its wine.

Communion requires more than
wine. Our trusting
must be shared, and, filling
both, it must just
be, beyond you or me,
transcendent of chalice and lips,
there: to drink infinitely.

Johns Hopkins, March 20, 1970

Arrangement

I have heard your hands
arranging fruit.

Our words in crystal compotes
lie like fruit too right, too ripe
to move.
L'exactitude n'est pas la vérité,
yet we would save the truth
in bowls.

I have watched your hands
arranging fruit.

We watch the bowl
create its rim, and like a mouth
contain itself.

The bowl I burden silently.
The fruit conforms:
an apple swells to red.

Arrangement:
with shapes inform the sense.
Informed, the apples acquiesce,
preserve the reddening
possibilities.

You draw
your hands away, blanched,
you, left to watch the truth,
you arrange the air.

Johns Hopkins, Spring 1970

Teaching Years in My 20s

*Thoughts arising when I taught English,
learning that my passion for literature and for others may be
unrequited*

As frequent as street corners in Holborn
are these chasms in the continuity of
our ways. Yet we keep straight on.
~ Virginia Woolf, Jacob's Room

I sit here
across from you
using the table
as a street corner.

the lamp grows into a
pole, your hand sprouts
vendor's flowers.
we are ready to speak,
you say. I block the
traffic out; the cars are
silent butlers, the noise
corralled in napkin rings.

it is silent, I think aloud.
but we are not alone; the
dogs of many dreams lope
toward us, drawn by the scent
of crumbs from what once
knew itself a table.

                    it is a street corner,

you say.

            yes, our conversation
could be casual, two sharing
life at street corners,

        but the dogs
circumlocute our selves, all selves,

our backstepping
hesitating selves, our early unkempt
selves, our silenced selves. They
smell our unknown selves,
ourselves unknown, and
seek us out and shed our
strangeness like irritable fleas
upon us—
        their sniffing delicately
proclaims mortality, and you and I,
at home again,
give them a bone.

National Council of Teachers of English, English Journal, May 1974

New Math

Then children, we confined our measures
to tables rounding out worn math books,
transforming pecks to bushels with innate abandon.

Memorizing tables, we measured
profits to infinities, and from both coasts
sped to the midland first by car,
then train, and plane, to test velocity.

We mastered decimals, reducing
wholes to fractions with a point,
for no point at all, and zero, as our
place-holder, fastened all configurations to a center.

Outgrowing math books while
growing older, we left those tables as
an epigraph to rationality. The
center has not held: the comfort gone
from circles rounding out their lines in
endless spheres.

Relationships we cipher now are
not proportional for new math. The world we compass calls
upon new formulas, rejects a rounding
off to nearest answers.

Our center pins its point where decimals repeat
in dizziness: irrationally certain.

1972

The gift from New York City

When my aunt and uncle returned from New York City
I always expected gifts. After all, they had no children,
and I was a child.

That one time, they gave me what I called a "motion" picture,
you know, the kind that is a photo placed beneath a wavy glass,
and everything starts moving when you rock it back and forth.
The woman in the picture beckons you, she stands on the
50th floor balcony of her high-rise in New York. Behind her,
lights blink on blink off with just a movement of my wrist,
so much more exotic than a tourist's postcard.

When my life would seem especially still,
I'd watch the woman on the balcony.
It seemed to me that even breezes
from that balcony embraced me then,
carrying me from my small bedroom,
from my small family,
from my small town
to New York
where I thought everything, even our darkest secrets and fears,
would be easier to live with
under those lights and at that height.

1970s

Last Visit

There were dust balls in every corner of her home, this
the immaculate home, now dingy,
a receptacle for dirt and clutter.

Blame it on her cancer. She had no energy for the Electrolux.

All I wanted to do was clean when I got there.
All I wanted was to take soft cloths, wipe gently around
all the antique cups and saucers.

Arrange all the cans in the pantry.

Move the furniture so that it looked like the floorplan of a
model home.

I took her sheets, smelling the tart sweetness of cancer,
pushed them into the washing machine,
rinsing them again and again.

I hung them on the clothesline stretched between the maple
trees, letting
the wet sheets fold around me, fragrant, smelling of May.

When I made my mother's bed, her sitting in the corner waiting to
lie down,
I'd smell the month, then smell her body.

Every evening I slept with her, her thinness folding itself into me as
if I were pregnant with her cancer, holding my breath as I held her.

Every morning the dust returned
as quickly as our pain.

1980

My Mother's Last Handbag

It is the last remnant I have of my mother's stuff,
what was left after we had given, sold, thrown out
the aftermath of death. I touch the coins for parking
meters, a plastic case for her driver's license, keys to her green
car, pictures of my brother and me, list of phone numbers
of "just in case" people, an old postcard from me from someplace
not Boston, and the last Rx with tablets that tried to banish pain.

The note I would have written a few years after she had died,
telling her about my divorce, would have been here, too,
carried around and worried over, problems
she liked to unravel like bad dates and allergies.

1980s

Antrobia culveri flourished here.
Today fewer than 150 are left. Runoff
from overgrazed pastures has washed
sediment and pollution into the creek's
once icy-clear waters, and is thought
to have killed off nearly all the snails.
~ Tumbling Creek Cave, MO

Bankrupt, divorced, Tom Aley,
so the story goes, creeps into caves,
spending his money,
losing his marriage,
looking for a blind snail,
haunted by its disappearance.

The *why* eludes us
until we remember how much
we hope that someone notices
our being missing
from tables, and chairs, and pictures
and groups and families,
from life.
We want others haunted
by our disappearance.

Tom Aley worries
"If you start losing
Pieces of the system,
It's all at risk."
One more *Antrobia culveri*

missing from its cave, and
one less person signing the guest book:
they both don't live here anymore.

1980

Parenthood, Divorce, Relationships

❦

New beginnings, some new endings, many new pathways

Revisiting the Aquarium

other visits had pressed her to the glass
tanks, the crowded halls inhaling space.

this time, her timing better, she used the halls
like estuaries, stopping, mooring, moving
slowly, fish to fish

to sense her kinship with these lives.

colors   changing as she had, piece by piece,
her life   camouflage   masking   as she'd done
in order to survive.

each loss
mother   father   brother
then husband   some friends   the years

so like the brittlestar, renewing from the stump
of grief a new arm,

she clasped herself, then him, and
reached the tanks in time for feeding.

*Monterey Bay Aquarium, CA 1990 – Published by Xavier
Review 1993*

A Solstice Solace

In the cold raw
that is winter,
warm to the facts that glow
like tapers that
in fifteen seconds
the moon will move
nine miles, that
Earth will measure more
by hundreds, that
a distant star will shine
for us millions
of miles in journey.
Let the birth of one child
the glimpsing of one star
all celestial motions
be present again to celebrate
ancient myths that have defined
this cold season
to be one
always
of beginnings.

Blink
before you the new measures of a year,
new seconds and minutes and hours
refining
refinding the last twelve months,
the lost meanings, the visions caught
between our lashes in
fifteen second frames.

Blink
and watch for new impressions,
quicken ·
the moving toward new time.

December 1994

Runaway

(after reading an Alice Munro story with the same title)

Maybe it is the very abstraction of all feelings,
making us trust in the simplicity of words like
runaway, and chance, soon and silence,
passion and trespasses, tricks and power,
until we think that maybe we can
board a bus and leave a life we never wanted to book,
until we disembark, returning to the bones of what we know
not what we may have wanted.
Or maybe it is finding a life that no one guessed we could slip into,
or maybe it is floating in a Chagall painting and losing our
drab dreams to color, eluding gravity for hope,
for keys to homes we've not yet found.
And then, maybe it's the silence that arises from old friends,
the ones you lose along the way,
not through death as much as through disuse.
Silence is the sound you need,
alone at the end of it all, tired of using your voice
when really all that's needed, at the end of it all,
is your whisper wondering what all this might have meant.

2001

Half-Hour

Coming out of sleep this morning, I hear the radio voice saying that there is at least one-half hour of a soap opera in everyone's life, and I think immediately of the two crows that have been pecking at my lawn all week, burrowing for grubs which transform themselves into Japanese beetles which I had seen this summer all over the outdoor walls of my home and had thought even then that maybe I was being invaded, that my life was an invitation for alien intrusions, but then the beetles disappeared and I continued in a state of heightened awareness of my posturing self. So now the crows come and the beetles have gone and the grubs which are their ending and beginning are somewhere in the tangled blades of grass beckoning to these crows to dig and dig and dig and when I come home from giving and giving and giving all day I see my lawn torn up and it reminds me of my being torn up because somehow you could not say that you would not burrow into my world anymore but just wanted to drift away, maybe for spiritual reasons (that's always a pure excuse) or because you needed more time for truth and beauty (thank you Keats), but maybe now the drifting is because we really had not common territory together and all there were were clumps of our lives like bits of sod torn up and thrown around, bits and pieces of me that were never *completely* understood, although I don't believe that we ever completely understand ourselves, let alone one another, and yet the crows and their caw caw-ing have settled upon this house and I found on the sidewalk a lost CD from some kid walking along my street from school and the label spoke of a band that was "40 shades of gray" and I wondered if indeed I had become so monochromatic that all color had left my life, that all I had was the crows but at least with the crows there is a bit of the soap opera in my life and that's worth at least a half-hour.

2001

54

Chinese Fortunes: Translations

- **Good beginning is half done.**
  Starting is rising from the pillow, remembering the dream, and recording the memory. First words give way to all words.

- **You will travel far and wide, both pleasure and business.**
  The short and long of it all has been cross-country and miles high and deep. The longest flight: reaching home after you had died just hours before. The shortest travelling: learning what travelling 'light' really means, and then riding with it.

- **You will pass a difficult test that will make you happier.**
  My tests have been as frequent as commas separating lists of words: eye tests to driving tests meant to measure some personal ability in a public way. Answering 'who are you, really?' and passing has given me my only happiness. No re-takes allowed.

- **No act of kindness, no matter how small, is ever wasted.**
  A little girl on my school bus sitting next to me threw up on our way home. I did not move, but sat next to her, trying to let her know that nothing could make her unacceptable. I cannot dry all of your tears, but one finger on your cheek, following the stream of one tear, lets me show I care and share sadnesses we both have.

- **The eyes believe themselves; the ears believe other people.**
  If I look upon myself with a jeweler's eyepiece, I see it all. The grainy defects and the shimmering radiance of maybes and is's. Like lightning, the vision comes before the thunder. In truth, I know myself before I hear you tell me who I am.

With insight, I listen to what I see, and understand what has
been said.

- **You are one of the people who 'goes places in life.'**
  At twenty, I thought that meant 'being on one's way' to fame
  and fortune. Decades later, I look closer to home for the places
  to visit. Soon, I imagine I will simply sit so that travelling
  far and wide can be deep and within. Then, I will have gone
  everywhere I must. Destination as ordination.

*Fall 2002, 2nd Prize, Common Ground's 2nd Annual Spiritual
Poetry Contest*

You're Wearing?
(the Oscar evening question)

Not Gucci, nor Dior, not any of the pleated, crimped, cinched,
rolling bolts of antique white, azure,
bisque, blanched almond,
cornsilk,
eggshell,
floral white,
Gainsboro, ghost white,
honeydew,
ivory, lavender, lavender blush, lemon chiffon, linen,
mint cream, misty rose, moccasin,
Navajo white,
old lace,
papaya whip, peach puff,
seashell, snow,
or thistle,
that all the stars are wearing this fragrant spring night.

I am remembering the talcum white of baby powder
I would sprinkle on my mother's peach puff chenille-wrapped body,
she, cowering on the carpet, crying glistening antique white tears,
looking up at my father, his face washed with Navajo white stubble,
his aging not tempering his anger, his alcoholic fuck you's
rising to my misty rose bedroom, staining the walls with wounded
tints, his words
her sobs
pulling me to grab what I knew as soothing, the sweet snow
of talc that would cloud the air, would banish blandness
would leave all of us new as babies.

And that I would carry the antique white container,
its papaya whip design, its azure letters,
downstairs to her,
sobbing a cry that still rises in my ears like cornsilk,
cheeks stained with tears, salty design of old lace,
I would sprinkle the powder over her,
imagining all colors leaving the living room
except for snow, except for that which could blanket
all harm,
conceal despair
and change my father's reddening self
to neutral hues.

Spring 2006

Canopic Jars

~~~Stoppered vases from the Greek name for
Canopus—they stored organs of the deceased that
were extracted during mummification~~~

Vase 1
Here is where my liver rests
in this human-headed
Amset's vase,
bile from bad conversations,
missed conversations,
words blackened from fighting.
In this vase,
slowly
I am learning
not to hear what you have not
said and not to understand what you
have not meant.

Vase 2
Here is where my intestines rest
in this falcon-headed
Kebeh-senu-ef vase,
coils of worrying, twisting trails.
All those one-way streets
and cul-de-sacs and
dead ends—a serpentine to
my saddest walks: away from old
loves, away from old hopes,
stumbling over my own entrails
in a pattern that confounded.
Slowly I am learning
to walk to the corner

and stop before I cross streets.

Vase 3
Here is where my stomach rests
In this jackal-shaped vase, Dua-mutef.
Nocturnal sadnesses, the times when
I most felt alone when I was most like
a scavenger for what I thought was right
for what I am learning to honor,
those deeds I perform that honor
myself.

Vase 4
Here is where my lungs rest
in this baboon-shaped vase, Hapi.
The doctor called the condition
consolidation of the lungs, this
pneumonia of my spirit,
and I grimaced, barely able to breathe,
spitting out, coughing out, words
that nobody wanted to hear.
Slowly I am learning to pull air
into these lungs, air from
inspiration, not from conspiracy.

Then will all of me rest.

Volume 5, 2007, The Importance of Water and Ash

Circus Girl

The circus girl, the one who could bend over
backwards, stare out behind her,
curl around under herself,
looks out towards disbelieving eyes
all wondering if they could replicate
her envied distortions.
The circus girl, the one who could bend over
backwards, curl around under herself,
moves her hands and pours a cup of tea,
fashioning herself
one large universe
of motion. She sips,
sighs now that her act is done.
The circus girl, the one who bends
forward in her dressing room
brushes her hair like a screen in front of her,
keeping out the circus for a moment.
Her upright world she wants to share, to tell
the others that she does take tea, does talk
does more than bend over backwards,
stare out behind her,
curl around under herself, look out towards
disbelieving eyes, those that marvel
at her precarious
balancing.
She wonders
if anyone would ever sit with her,
pour tea with her,
talk with her,
unfold sounds to her

as she stretches, unbends herself,
stands up to who she is unbound.

2007

7 Lies I Have Told

I remember most the six-foot scarf Miss Grady
helped me tie around my neck one wintry day
my being merely six and clumsy with the tying of a bow, and
then her question wound so tightly round my neck, the,
"Does your mother tell you that you're pretty?" curled
itself up to my ears. So easily did it begin, my variations on
the truth
with my replying "no," not wanting to appear
too satisfied with how I looked that I preferred to tell Miss
Grady "no."
And so began the lies. Small at first, like telling mother
I had liked the dress she bought me, yes, but really, no, and
telling my piano teacher·I would be fine *sans* music sheets
on our recital eve, yes, but really no,
and telling my dear diary pages that Jimmy liked me best of all
the girls,
yes, but really,
no.
Then the lie to Josephine about my father,
"Does he live with you?" and yes,
when, really, no, and then the lie to George about my
gastronomic wit, not knowing vichyssoise was cold potato soup, but
smiling yes when really, no, and for the seventh I will share
with you
the time I said he hadn't hurt me no, when really, yes and yes
and yes.

Summer 2010

A Marriage and a Garden

Kneeling is a prelude to our prayer
The task of weeding soul and soil required
for gardens that are more than lupine layers

We rid the yard of goldenrod and snare
the leafy spurge and thistles reaching higher
since kneeling is a prelude to this prayer.

And hauling stones to build these rustic stairs
was your gift to your first bride's green desires
for gardens that were more than lupine layers

And now this marriage for us new and fair
has beckoned us with chimes of floral choirs
that kneeling is a prelude to pure prayer

So on our knees we pull and prune and tear
those weeds of spurge and sorrel and despairs
since weeding soul and soil is what's required

For this a seedling marriage needs soul care
and soil that's rich with who we truly are
since weeding soul and soil has been required
to make our kneeling prelude to our prayers.

August 2010

For a brother lost

(with thanks to Charles Baudelaire)

So much of you is yanked from memories, pulled from this or that
one, snaking
like the 'whip' of children's games where I hold out my hand for
yours and you're not
there. There's one that drizzles images of you in borrowed clothes
and shadowed grief
wandering through the funeral home, already shedding brother
from your tongue,
moving toward a future without mom, moving farther from the
sister you chose not to see.
That day you told yourself *I'm not my sister's brother* you
pledged yourself familial amnesia: no answers needed as to why you
did not graduate, were
fired, had not learned to drive—your residence became an
unknown place these 30 years.
That this year marks the 30th that I mark intake sheets with *no
living siblings* startles as much
as saddens me. I wonder if you've married, where you live, whose
paths you transect daily three thousand miles from me; I wonder
who you've come to look like. The ease with which I've found a
probable address for you is but a mask for the unease with which
I've tried to write to
you; what do I say but *why* and *why* and *why* to you for all the days
and months and years
we've lost. How hard it must have been to be my brother, me who
always seemed to get life

'right' and you who veered away from base paths and home plate and simply ran away from any and all games. How little of the rules we understood. No games, this letter I might send, but hands outstretched to you, beginning with "dear brother."

Summer 2010

Life's to film as

Somewhere between the previews, prequels,
and short takes, anticipation's patina appears. I
settle into darkened popcorn comfort somewhat
ready for the partly unexpected
trials and travails this heroine will
greet. If art's the lie that tells the truth
(my memory serves up Picasso's words)
I'm learning how to cloak my life in
fiction's chasuble, wear well-embroidered truths
that cloak the plot I've learned to live, and
with the taking of a cinematic wafer
I watch the hours of someone else's life and
swallow well the holy epilogue that only
years from now will tell me if I got it right.

Summer 2010 ~ Published in Ekphrastic California.

Why does this happen to me?

It had gotten to the point that my record was **"restaurants burned down, boarded up, bandaged with announcement strips of 'closure, bankruptcy, or relocation' = 5"** vs.
"still available love relationships = 0." Any time "we" (the current *you and me*) had frequented any of our culinary haunts, I began to suspect that soon *that* restaurant would cease to exist about the time that *we* would, too. Another of "our" restaurants, I thought, from the local list, one we'd pick after sleeping in on Saturdays. The last one, the one with *huevos rancheros,* the smell of kitchen lard threading the air and stitching itself to our nostrils, I'd actually relished—kind of how I cared for you. But meals closed like our hearts, just like all those sets of stainless I'd wind up with, minus at least one knife.

New Year's Eve
He had asked me to come about the time of hors d'oeuvres, about the time the host and hostess would be circulating making introductions, making small talk the size of one-bite morsels that keep you sated until you don't want the main meal. Not that he hadn't found himself saying 'couple' when we were together. No, that wasn't it at all. He just didn't want to end one year, start another, with the assumption we were together. Clean slate, he said. Let's use New Year's Eve as a trial balloon—why not both come as individual invitees, then find each other over a drink, perhaps sit down together, maybe even break bread together? That way, no one would assume we were a couple. We were individual courses—not the 3-course meal. Anyway, I knew he always thought *prix fixe* was still too much money for a meal.

Smudge Pots

It had gotten cold enough for smudge pots, but there was an art to getting them to work well—and there was a temperature she needed to watch for, one where she could open the holes on the control top to get more heat to the fruit trees. Today, it seemed as if her fingers had frozen as well as the fruit. Nothing she did worked. The smudge pots tonight were finally lighted, well *after* the temperature had dropped below 25 degrees—and the small chimneys were vertical sentinels that wound up guarding nothing. Tomorrow, there would be the sadness, the losses, the faint smell of the beginning of ripening overtaken by the smell of grieving smoke that hadn't warmed anything. She would feel cold for a while; she would hear cold from the others; she would live cold, it was possible, forever.

Summer 2010

A woman giving birth to herself

Perhaps the hardest moments of my life at 32 were the ones spent lying with my dying mother, feeling her giving birth to her dying, feeling myself giving birth to my losing her. The prior two years had seen me giving birth to my first son, and my mother and I had worn well our new roles. This first grandchild, even 3,000 miles away in California, provided my mother with the new life that her long separation from my father and her later struggles with cancer had halted. In the most quiet moments of those early mornings that only distant trucks and trains own, I would lie quietly with my mother, my being back in Boston again, letting her dying body fill that space between my womb and her back. I felt myself giving birth to myself as my mother's only daughter, now a mother myself, and now giving birth to this new phase of life which would not include the woman who had given me life. And the questions tumbled about me, challenging me to find out how to ask them. How would life be without my mother's presence? How would I ever answer those questions for which I had thought, for years, only my mother knew the answers?

A woman giving birth to herself

It was in that home, my family home, that the 8-year old version of me had wondered if I would ever know who I truly was. Why, I had even stopped to look to my mother for an answer when my Aunt Lottie had asked me whether I wanted a banana or an orange during one of our family dinners. I wasn't sure I knew the answer—which fruit meant more to me, which had, for my palate, a more satisfying flavor? That was it—flavors were mysteries to me. My mother—delightful, bright, witty—was my ideal. She had all the traits I craved. Ironically, though, I slowly grew afraid to be my own taste-tester. Like the court-appointed protector of the royal family, my mother had taken upon herself the role of testing the world before I sampled it. Then came dancing classes and junior high school—new worlds where I thought I could ingest a new self for myself, or, hopefully, at least join the world a little more fully.

A woman giving birth to herself

Dancing classes—I was sure that I was the only girl whose mother refused to let her wear her hair 'down' during ballroom dancing lessons where my long-haired girlfriends would eye the 8th grade boys who would soon be our dance partners for the evening. My long brown hair was typically pulled back, tied with a bow or barrette, never able to flow as I'd imagined the streaming tresses of an Austen or Bronte heroine would. I remember the evening I arrived at Piety Corner (yes—that was the name of the ballroom dancing venue in our little New England town) with my hair cut and styled. And then, the comments…"We loved your long hair!" "Why did you get it cut?" My internal monologue told me that, indeed, my new hairdo was the paradoxical result of my trying to make a statement, but the statement was simply my longing to be different, to live a life imagined by me and not someone else. But I hadn't understood that it was not the outward semblance that needed styling; it was the interior life and small voice that cried to be set forth, naked and free to the world, to affirm my intuition of who I was becoming physically and emotionally: a wonderful, if slowly emerging, prelude to Barbara.

A woman giving birth to herself

College—a place where I must have hit the mute button for a few years, so absolutely terrified was I of all the women who were attending this very privileged college. An author writing about my Wellesley class later dubbed us "rebels in white gloves" and I suppose we were a concoction of outspoken rebellion as well as demure manners. After all, hadn't I the repository of etiquette lessons at my mother's home, the correct fork and knife positions, the correct conversational menus from which to draw? I clearly saw myself as someone who was learning to speak up, but the voice emerging was so soft that only those close by could hear the whispered thoughts I pushed out, contraction by contraction, to my college world. An English professor of mine asked me if I was going to be able to lead the class, as all of us were required to do. I hesitated, saying I wasn't sure if I had comprehended all of Milton's nuanced writing, nor gleaned the sources of all his classical allusions. Ms. Lever said, "Ask questions of the text; the answers will rise up eventually—but learn to ask questions first." I did. Milton had written *The mind is its own place, and in itself/Can make a heaven of hell, a hell of heaven (Paradise Lost)*. I began to ask questions of myself and resisted the feeling of being someone whose mind had seemed internally trapped inside my head; I began to give birth to a woman who was learning to ask questions.

A woman giving birth to herself

Against a backdrop of white snow, the flame-colored floor-length winter coat I had bought was like a struck match. I was in New England at an all-girls' private boarding school, teaching Thomas Hardy's The Mayor of Casterbridge. I remember Lucetta Templeman as a woman who, over time, gave birth to herself, making choices as wisely as she could, given the restrictions of her time and her means. I remember looking out at the small gatherings of girls on this rolling campus near the Connecticut River, marveling at the many choices I felt that women in the early 70s had, and wondering, as I made impressions in the snowy walks I took the two winters I taught there, if I were going to be choosing wisely between my flickering hopes for love and career, for writing and motherhood, for East coast and West Coast. On a muggy summer day, I packed up my red coat, having resigned from Northfield's faculty, moved to Boston, and settled into the next two years that would serve as a prelude to my gestation of coming to life as a woman. Ahead of me, relishing my teaching the written words of Thoreau and Emerson at a public high school, thriving on words that encouraged renewal and rebirth. In the process, probably in the last metaphorical trimester of my gestation period, I renewed my connection with my mother who, by this time, could see me distinctly and uniquely. No longer the filter for my world, she had allowed me to sew the shadow back onto myself so that, like Peter Pan, I actually cast one.

A woman giving birth to herself

It is now three decades later and I sit here writing about "a woman giving birth to herself." The phrase came back to me recently when one of my college friends who is struggling with cancer was described by another classmate as 'always being a woman giving birth to herself.' I liked the sound of the phrase and I believe I can describe myself that way now. Before, no—I was not ready to 'own' this phrase. But now, having survived the loss of my mother, the birth of my second son, the loss of my marriage, and my recent re-marriage at age 61, I am surveying the landscapes that I've traversed. I think the red coat of my youth, long ago given away, has stayed with me as an emblem of my wanting to be noticed. I think the questions of my college days have become not obstreperous, but simply spoken aloud. I think the very name I was given at birth, *Barbara*, which means "stranger, foreigner," has brought me comfort when I have understood myself to be neither stranger nor foreigner to the extended families that, over the past three decades, have cared for me and my sons. Now, as the very feminine essence of myself realizes that giving birth is not an option for this last part of my life, I realize I am a woman who has given birth to herself as an invigorating presence, questioner, partner, mother. I am the one who can be seen at a distance, through many woods, walking deliberately into a clearing, ready to give birth to herself as I now lie down in green pastures, as I now walk *deeper and deeper/into the world,/determined to do the only thing I could do—/determined to save/the only life I could save (The Journey, Mary Oliver)*. I am ready for the seasons, for my winter moments, eager to wear a red coat once more, my emergence as a woman giving birth to herself, nearly complete.

Spring 2010

Do you lilac it?

I'm standing in front of a hundred small bottles with a color spectrum staring back, but it's the colors' titles on the bottom of the bottles that ultimately make me choose what I'll want brushed on my nails. I'm thinking about the first time I smelled nail polish, that nostril-widening experience of ethyl acetate that, like its predecessor thousands of years ago in China, transformed ordinary fingernails into artistic experiences. My first time with nail polish was when I was a little girl, and my mother painted my nails a bright red, courtesy of the Coty bottle that stood on her dresser, ready to make her nails look special for special occasions, opened for me when I had dance recitals. Scott and Dorothy Douglas were the big names in my small town for dance instruction, and Dorothy had named me Miss South America for my first big recital—my costume with the long net sleeves and red and green and yellow spangles on them—and my fingernails dipped in that Coty ruby red. I loved the smell of nail polish like I loved the smell of gasoline and lighter fluid, something almost dangerous about them, but also necessary. Like filling up your car, or throwing lighter fluid on the charcoal, nail polish was something I thought of as part of growing up—something that involved a bit of risk, but also part of developing a style.

Not surprisingly, I always wanted to wear nude or clear color, not the deep red that the 3000 BC upper-class women of China would have worn. I knew that we were not rich, and red tinted nails seemed to me destined for my stage appearances and not for social occasions. Clear, lacquered, polymer nails were the color-chart choice, always on the side of under-stated. Funny that now, standing in front of a hundred small bottles, I remember my Aunt Lilly, who was not really an aunt but one of my mother's close friends and seemed related to Jean Harlow. Lilly was a platinum blonde woman who always seemed to have the longest nails, the reddest polish, and a penchant for having everything around her gilded—clothing, couches, car, life.

I'm reading the bottom of the bottles—I like "Worth a pretty penne," a subtle shade, not too obvious, or "Be there in a prosecco," with its hint of the blush of a light wine. I am years away from the little girl in the recital, but cannot, still, bring myself to try the red fingernail polish, thinking it a bit too much of an attention-getter. That thirty-five-cent bottle of Coty nail polish is still on my mother's bureau in my mind as I think of her heading to Woolworth's to get one more bottle to make sure there is enough for my dance recital—I'll have my toes painted even though they're under my tap shoes.

My brother's walking towards me, looking like an unshaven lost soul, and I want to be as far away as I can be in this funeral home, in another of the parlors, not near my mother's casket, not near him, not near the lines of people that want to pay respect to my mother—her former students, her neighbors, her siblings who stand like sentinels near her, quiet guardians for their younger sister. I'm thinking that I should have had a manicure, that I should have checked with the undertaker to see how my mother's hands were, that, at the very end, I should have made sure that her nails were tended, at the least, with something like "A Rose at Dawn"—something red, something special.

Summer 2010

And, Other Writings

❦

over these recent and distant years
my meanderings into art and heart
the refrains becoming familiar
never old

The Voice Not Heard

was often mine, the girl who sat so still, legs crossed,
head down, exhausted from the swallowing of sound,
the hidden alphabet for all those words not uttered,
and so I sat, so still,
imagining what I might sound like if I'd had a voice
to call out answers to what happened on page forty-three,
or who had disappeared before the chapter's end. So shy, the only
sounds I'd make some days were sighs.
Older now, I've left that silent room.
I birthed my voice, called forth a
me who sounded throaty and poetic and secure,
who'd call attention to myself and shriek and yell and carry on
and finally answer who I was aloud
to anyone who'd listen.

2011

Head of a Woman:
Dora Maar, March 28, 1939

My private muse. Attributed to Pablo Picasso

Long before I saw you, I had pictured me.
After I had seen you, I pictured us.
That first encounter, *Les Deux Magots,*
I took my hand, stretched it on our cafe table,
jabbed between each finger with my knife,
an act that fascinated me, and drew you in.
The Dora series shows my eyes gaze here and there,
staring into space to points unknown,
holding your gaze, my lover. In the portrait I loved most,
the Dora three years into loving you,
you had me wear the burnt sienna top
you said smelled like the pungency of passion.
The labyrinthine necklace whorled its way,
unlike you, to the center of my heart;
the beryl background you provided
pushed me from you, to the darkest berm of being,
to my vanishing point, which you encouraged me to do
a few years later.

Fall 2015 ~ Published in Ekphrastic California December 2015

Cezanne: Still Life with Skull

On loan at the National Gallery, Washington, D.C., 1970s

So
the skull
ensnares
you, too.
      As flesh assigned
to stopper
bungholes stops
the mind, you too
assigned the skull
its space
      and for all time
you placed
      the base of thought
            and dream
atop a book.
      I nod,
      agree.
         Words could be
         my death.

Johns Hopkins, 1970 ~ published 2015 in Ekphrastic California

Photoshopping

It's the picture I think of when I think "mother, young," before
she had her own unhappy marriage, before I was "in the picture,"
the formal portrait of her sister's wedding, the family gathered,
arranged, like the marriage, for this sitting. It's the picture she took
out to show me, always, what she had looked like before her parents
were "out of the picture": the unsmiling bride, the serious groom,
the somber portrait of a family whose daughter had been given to
another family's son for the portrait of a good marriage. It's the
picture with the missing portrait, the person behind my mother
who was manipulated out of the scene, just as the bride and groom
had been manipulated into it. It's the scratched lines, the dodging,
it was called, the lightening above my mother's head that always
takes my eyes away from bride and groom and uncles and mother.
Who was the person who did not make the cut, who remains in
smudged extinction as part of the wedding portrait? A suitor of my
mother's? A person who had vied for Aunt Sophia's hand but had
not won? Someone who fit the phrase "damnatio memoriae"—dis-
honoring somehow this immigrant family who'd made America
its home, not unlike the Roman who'd been condemned to nil.
Sometimes I wish I had the magic to airbrush memories, remove
that boyfriend, forget that date, expunge that divorce, forget
that colleague, conversation, trip, party, exchange...until I realize
retouched photos give the wished for, not the lived. That wedding
photo had been taken, developed, changed. All I can do is wonder
why, remembering we cannot change the past.

2016

speak falsely, tell an untruth,

Late 12C., from Old English legan, ligan, earlier leogan
deceive, belie, betray

in this poem there are no lies,
falsetto voices, maybe, but no deceit.
in this poem, there are no lies,
receding hairlines, maybe, but not bald-faced barrages
like the stories that my father spoke,
coming home so rarely that **that** truth overtook all lies,
and we were told to say 'our father' like the prayer,
'who art not in heaven and who isn't home,'
is never home will never be home does not want to be home,
in this world there are no lies. Like the time the doctor told
my mother
she had time left, prescribed her meds
for numbered days, when her days were numbered,
and in that moment in that hospital,
there were no lies, just her hearing
just enough from morphine dreams there might be hope
of maybe one more lunar movement,
one more time, this waxing and this waning of the truth.
in this poem there're no eclipses of the truth,
just different ways to tell a lie,
legan, ligan,
the truest stories that my parents couldn't bear to hear nor say.

Fall 2015 ~ Published in Hartskill Review 2015

Tyne/tine

I

In her dream, she tends the argument,
her sounds, tipped, sharp prongs to stab at meaning.
Earlier, she'd dined on galantine, and moved the
mounded meat around to change the shape
of dinner. It bothered her, this wounded
meandering, the travels to clandestine scabs
she could not scrape away.

II

The headstone maker needed dates for birth and death,
the hyphens two sides: a place card for her mom's
last meal, engraved in travertine,
her mother seated at a table
set for one.

III

When young, she learned to set the altar for her church;
Christ's meal for all she placed upon the patine,
the wheaten circles offered for communion,
a feeding with no need for forks:
cupped hands receive the bread;
the meal's eternal promise pressed into each palm.
A meal meant to be savored in one moment.

IV

Her father's anger bruised her, felt as sharp as if he'd taken tines
and prodded her, a routine not unknown; the dining'd not gone
well and soon the meal had ended, both sides jabbing back,
the mounted tres-tine looking at the words that flew between
the two: the meaning cleared away, no courses left to share,

she swallowed down the meal with bitters, following the Tyne
to sea,
dreaming that she'd slept through dinner,
longing for a ship where all who cared
would be on board.

Summer 2015 ~ Published in Boston Accent

Path to Tupelo Point at Wellesley College

There is a point a vanishing point a point beyond the promontory
an indentation on the page beneath the page you've pressed
your pencil and it's this point where you begin
to go back go deep go farther than you've dared to
to that moment near a tree, a topilwa, swamp tree, genus Nyssa,
an inky tree, residing at the point where the Tupelo meets water,
where girls were wooed, proposed to, and then wed.
Your point, though, leaves that point and takes you back to
former points
where you had thought of vanishing yourself, not ready
to pronounce
your name, but only that you were an ingenue, naïf, fair maiden
who sang *O Thou Tupelo thou hast a certain magic charm,*
the evensong that flowed from opened o's of mouths
and you're aware of sounds no words just sounds
clues where to walk, where breadcrumb lyrics take you
to Tupelo to the point where land vanishes into water and roots
tunnel to
memories you've pointedly forgotten. You seek the ritual
of repetition the sound of rustling the singing of old songs that
even now
return to you the old refrains, the lilac trees, the bridal wreaths, the
floral framing
of the points that still you, quiet you, make you wonder where the
young man is,
the one who said he'd not forget the point he'd made at Tupelo
when fragrant promises could make the hawthorn bushes disappear.

Fall 2015

*"It is possible that the power of
the work is enhanced by the very
fact the head is missing."*
The Winged Victory of Samothrace, Wikipedia

Her wings fan backwards, her arms are gone, and we,
as if we felt the same winds, push ahead to walk around this
stillness, walk around the marble folds, the windy helm
of some ship, somewhere, staring at this headless icon.

I am reminded of those times when I imagined movement,
grew limbs so I could leave, but often fluttered frozen in my place:
our conversation heavy, a pedestal of stone the base of all we'd force
ourselves to say: a solitude unwelcomed, undesired.

A brokenness unable to be mended.

Those times my wings, like hers, would noisily attempt escape,
eventually descend to my own marbled feet, pinioned in
my desperate
need for love, trapped by all my heart had told my head.

A staircase to another room of treasures, these with heads and arms,
yet we glance back to see our Nike, imagining her limbs,
her head, imagining ourselves, like her, survivors of our storms.

Fall 2015 ~ Published in OASIS JOURNAL 2017

Prestidigitators

Front row seats promised us the chance
to figure out the trick behind the tricks, the customary
rabbit from the hat, the infinite unraveling scarf, the severed rope
no longer wispy frays but whole.
A pause:
the slender sleight-of-hand man now asks
if there's a watch
to offer up, oblation for his act.
You, just eight, implore me to give up my watch, the one
that marks time as the Swiss have promised.
I look around to see if someone else is buying in, and I am saved,
another's watch is offered, smashed, and reappears on someone
else's wrist.
It doesn't matter now, if silver balls float
to mid-air, or coins appear from ears,
or even if the magic man
escapes the tank of water. You see only that
I couldn't trust, and I leave tasked with finding where
the magic went when years ago my mother
tried to bring my father back, his having disappeared
a final time.

Fall 2015 ~ Published in OASIS JOURNAL 2018

No Through Traffic

Anticipating coffee, and now just bits of conversation,
like the image the barista makes with foam, swirling quickly, gone,
my friend who has dementia sits and smiles.
She can't remember what she did the last few days,
nor if she has enough to eat at home, but she remembers clearly
years ago
the college literary magazine she had dubbed
Cul-de-Sac
the place where all her friends' unpublished work
could find a home, not the dead ends they'd
found at other journal sites. So here,
we talk about the Cul-de-Sac,
its paradox not unseen by me,
her sitting in the cafe's corner, in a new impasse
where words gathering in her throat
appear instead as tears,
new syllables she substitutes
for what she can't imagine how to say.

Summer 2015

The value of forgetting,
the lure of reinvention…
~ Nightingale, Kristin Hannah

※

I thought, "heart," fingering the worn-down beach rock
I probably shouldn't have taken
the day we'd climbed down sand dunes to the water's fringe,
my wanting the day's theme to be love, connection, touching
like the smooth heart-shaped rock that fit so easily into my hand.
The day had rules; you'd said we'd needed time, space, this day.
I forgave old conversations, waited for new words
I seemed to lose as sea sounds carried off what we said.

※

Years later, planting bulbs, gently nestling
the grape hyacinth, the calla, gladiolus, the daffodils into soil
we'd worked on making rich,
I found the heart rock found so many years before.
I think I'd planted it, as seed, hoping it would help us
grow all tangled in each other's care,
maybe even able to utter love. Instead, as I

looked up which bulbs do well in spring,
the tulips, daffodils, the crocus and iris breaking through,
I found as many that do not.

Summer 2016

Forms

Form found at the New York Public Library, April 2016

My___(Noun)___has ever belonged to you,
Will___(Adverb)___be yours,
beyond this ___(Noun)___even,
there beside you as you___(Verb)___,
and___(Verb)___,
and ___(Verb)___, and
___(verb) out a window.

Version I

My incomprehension has ever belonged to you,
Will probably be yours,
beyond this life even,
there beside you as you strayed,
and wandered,
and traipsed, and
drifted out a window.

Version 2

My sadness has ever belonged to you,
Will intermittently be yours,
beyond this reality even,
There beside you as you forsook,
and disavowed,
and revoked, and
nullified out a window.

Summer 2016

How much time...

My Kindle shows 8 minutes left of reading
8 minutes of threading through the black and white of words
illuminated technically from some inner source. Magic, I ask
myself, how does it know I have 8 minutes left to read about
the ravages of war, rejection by one's parent, hunger that growls
beyond one's stomach and makes me ravenous and guilty all
at once.
What if I spend more time to understand what these specks mean
in light of all that happens in one chapter of one's life? What if
the 8
becomes a 10 or 12 or more? What if I simply pause and still
the reading,
so my processor, beset by lack of agile electronic speed, my
brain, can
stop the stream of words to simply wonder why
what's happened has.
Ingenious Kindle.
It resets all, still shows 8 minutes left to reach an ending to
the horrors
that subside but do not stop for those where war seeps into
other volumes.

Summer 2016

Super Moons

entered my lexicon when one loomed,
hung, irradiated my sky one night
it seemed I'd driven
straight into the moonset of a screen lot,
as I imagined the 30% brighter, 14% larger
moon flooding my brain, that organ desperate
to create moon illusions that let the milky orb
sit plumply on my horizon. More than moons, though,
this one led me to think about what illuminates,
what exposes all that lies beneath it, beneath us,
all those neglected parts of our worlds,
the neighbors not spoken to for years,
the family members on the 'outs' with us, the fellow
elevator riders we parallel in stance,
the travelers we sit next to silently,
the beggars we avert, the edges of
all lives we somehow manage, sometimes, to avoid.
A super moon says 'no'—look, watch, I've exposed
what you need to see.

And, I must say, so have you. You've led
me to reflect more on ancient scripts that lead to modern tales,
you've asked me to divest myself of trappings that conceal,
invest myself with values that reveal the alabaster moments
coloring a world of many hues with love, with grace, with joy,
a spectrum created not by absence but by presence, my presence,
your presence, our allowing us to feel the pull of gravity towards
each other, hoping we can mimic perigee, stay close, stay near
no matter how far apart we are. The world calls us to stay
with.

2016

To Edward Albee, Summer 2016

You don't know this, that I wrote about you spring
of 1968, the year I took Modern Drama, and found you,
posted on our syllabus, near Miller and O'Neill and Williams,
read you, had your plays move into my life well after that
spring term.
I know you've passed from this world—maybe to another—
but I want you to know, anyway, you made the words I use,
the words I choose to hear, the words of others,
more intimate, intimidating, inimical, nearing
amicable, but always veering towards our terrible truths,
the ones that make us want to plunder
as well as pleasure each other. Your words made me understand
what the lady
from the League of Women Voters said explaining
California's propositions,
"Everything has unintended consequences"—
I believe her, and you.
All your characters trying to teach each other what life in the raw
might be,
beyond platitudes, beyond rituals, beyond roles.
All my characters, I now think, tried to teach me how to live
with loss,
listening to break-ups phoned in from a payphone, or watching
furniture divvied
up until my living spaces breathed relief.
So much space there is between us, you'd say, and yet all of us,
your characters, my characters, crowd in as if there is a secret that
we want to hear
but realize, at the last, that many of our utterances are mime.

2016

A Thesaurus for Legislators

...the opposite of a dictionary...you turn to it when you have the meaning already but don't yet have the word. It may be on the tip of your tongue, but what it is you don't yet know. You know well enough that the other words you try out won't do. They haven't the punch or have too much. They are too flat or too showy, too kind or too cruel...so you reach for the Thesaurus.

~I. A. Richards

Who are the poets, Shelley asked, if not the world's "unacknowledged legislators," and that leads me to wonder what do poets legislate, enact, make happen, what do they dream of, envision, hope for, why are they unacknowledged, unnamed, unknown, and what would they think of politics today, with promises of jobs and walls and isolation and renaming and remaking the reworking of the American dream so all can participate in being legislators of their future, with debate becoming badinage, and badinage becoming words one chooses to ignore, and slowly, surely, certainly, there is at times, no, often, no light at the end of the candidates' tunnels, and conventional wisdom seems so far away from Enlightenment that while we may be closer to the Romantics, our expressions veering toward the personal, rarely do they pass as healing, we can say definitely, with some definition, this, our new humanity, is not ready to be signed off as legislation without poetic license.

Summer 2016

What was it about the start of school and autumn poems?

They all seemed descendants of the ones
the year before, poems filled with the oranges and yellows
and mapled seasons, rhyming and sounds making
memorizing easier, so our teacher said:
> red and dead
> and flower head
> embedded sounds within my head,
> pursued by pall and sprawl,
> and finally, once and for all,
> the last leaf's fall.

Each stanza a die-cut stamp of swirling
words waiting for the harvest of recitation day.

Not ever was I able to perfectly proclaim my autumn
poem but after school let out, I'd take the long way home,
those autumns in New England, marveling at leaves
above   below   around,
remembering how green was used for cover up
and red, the leaf's food, trapped like words
in my closed throat
through winter, spring, and summer
> until the fall
> and my attempt to recall
> what really mattered
> all in all.

2016

Mezze

Finished with the crossword puzzle, I turn to food,
the section headlines small and savory.
T'mazza: savor in little bites.
It's what my daybook beckons,
nibble on these little thoughts,
perhaps to whet your writing appetite?
All my inserts, clippings, phrases take me back
to Warsaw 2017, bits and pieces of the world we'd flown across,
laid out platters of green Fiesta ware on blue tablecloths, my notes
remembering the days before Ash Wednesday, when Poles use up
the last of butter, the last of sugar, before they fast. But now I'm
feasting on the mezze of my notes, why I collected notes on Paczki,
soft and dense, filled dough with rose hip jam, filled me enough
to last
through Lent. I sample more, return to mezze, now the notes
take me
to time-lapse feeds, a link to Ahwahnee Meadows, I can
watch a full day in 40 seconds, time lapsing, then
wash down this sampler with my entry of the Dutch word *verlof,*
furlough, first meaning permission, now giving me time,
suspended
between what I read and write and do,
time to sample more of mind
figuring out what might matter.
Mezze, always, before this and other meals.

2017

Driving Home

...what I was called upon to do, me,
the niece as navigator, uncle driving in the front seat,
aunt, mother, brother, all of you, in the back,
our Sunday driving to New Hampshire drove
us to the border of uncertainty.
The maps' own folds could hide our destination,
the dot removed that should have been our city.
I learned that reading maps was easier than reading feelings, sensing
tensions creased between my aunt and uncle, mother and aunt.

Later, another drive, this time with you,
searching for Four Corners, finding that medallion seal,
thinking as we stepped on every quadrant
I was truly nowhere in your life
and maybe both of us had not found a place in mine.

We were sitting, you and I,
on plastic-covered seats
those muggy summer days
stuck in one position,
trying to unpeel our legs,
trying to figure grace into our leaving.

Those were the car stories I'd remember
but it took years for me to understand
the endless Sunday drives with family,
trying to be family,
and then the trips with you,
trying to belong,
and finally driving with myself,

finding it all right to be
in the driver's seat, finally driving home.

2017 ~ Winner, 2nd Place, Writing it Real Poetry Contest

Crazing

Odd, pursued by that bowl, the one I couldn't stop seeing,
its infinite craze lines like the vessels in a blood-shot eye
finding me throughout the day I'd spent perusing pottery,
a day when frayed threads of broken conversations followed me
from shelf to shelf, from booth to booth, the potters' work
reminders that containers sometimes don't contain, and
pitchers cannot pour.
              Desired by the potter, crazing's fine,
extending arteries with melting and then fusing glass on clay,
the movements push the viewer to see
                              more than color, more than line.
But it's the unintended crazing pulling me today,
the lines on that one bowl I'll probably go buy,
the one that was an accident, the crazing going on
for years beyond the firing.
              What I'll remember
when I see it on my table, linear landscape in an earthen bowl,
are all the lines I've heard again, once more, rephrased, reframed,
the ones that drove me crazy when I thought I knew what
others meant
and found I only knew what they had said.

Spring 2017 ~ Published in OASIS JOURNAL 2017

> *"Probably the best thing to do is not to get lost."*
> Boy Scout Handbook, 1940 Edition

Finding home's a labyrinthine matter,
a seeking of the origin of utterance and tale,
a sorting through of family noise and clatter.

A compilation of the photos that one's gathered
in images both subtle and pronounced that wail:
finding home's a labyrinthine matter.

Beginnings begat endings, visuals of chapters,
births divorce and postludes speak in images like Braille:
a sorting through of family noise and clatter.

Vows made relinquished to vows battered
the comings and the goings of a family's tale.
finding home's a labyrinthine matter.

Who disappeared, deserted, scattered
as family separated into journeys that entailed
a photo compilation of family noise and clatter.

For all dissension quieted in imagery's patter,
the photos that depict the family's vale.
A sorting through of family noise and clatter.
Reaching home's a labyrinthine matter.

2017

Upon Seeing "Nude in the Box"

Light is my inspiration, my paint and brush.
It is as vital as the model herself.
~ Ruth Bernhard, photographer of "Nude in the Box" 1962

To be certain, there are those days,
the ones too filled with doings,
when I feel laid to rest, boxed
like Bernhard's nude, reclining, restricted,
not able to stretch myself beyond the edges
obligations draw. Why move when movement
finds itself constrained? Why try to stand
when horizontal planes arrest
the impulse to arise?
There is the slightest yearning in this nude, her arm
extended just beyond her head, grasping
space beyond the box
for what might lie beyond. For me,
when I can glimpse the corner of my life
beyond my captive self, I am inclined to toss
and turn, to rotate to the perpendicular,
to let my arms and legs propel me beyond
shadows, to unencumbered light that paints
away the darkness of a life at times
too busy to see beyond.

Spring 2017 ~ Printed online in The Ekphrastic Review 2020

Communion with Dementia

Today you prefaced your remarks as
maybe I'd think them crazy, but here they are,
you'd smile before you shared
your neighbor had strung a clothesline
to your bedroom where she rappels
to take your clothes
and then you stop and say a word or two to
someone hovering nearby, not visible to us.
I listen, think about the mornings when I walk from room to room
forgetting why I've come and gone, think of the strands
of conversations that, like strands of silver hair that fall into my
eyes, fall
waywardly, wandering from meaning, far from order, think
about the interrupted dreams I forage, pillow scraping at my face,
grasping dreams evaporating into other tales
most likely taken from the chapter I'd last read,
the mystery that we'd watched the night before. I wonder
as I look at you, my friend with your dementia, not knowing how
to use
your plastic knife but knowing that your hair's not combed, how
much alike
we are, both souls who wish to make our days and nights
have meaning
as we sip our coffee, these Starbucks chairs like pews,
beseeching some divinity
to save us from communion with life's sadness, life's truth
that memories are fallible, that our realities shift endlessly,
until we start to understand the paradox that we can live
and not live all at once,

but most of all, we learn to savor what communion means
if we are only left to taste the crumbs.

2017

I seem to be floundering in a
sea of metaphor ~ but I hope
you grasp my meaning.
Jerusha Abbott, Daddy-Long-Legs

In truth, a table,
not a sea, the hands around not deckhands
but fingers grasping lines, not rigging, not to sails,
but to books that lay like lifeboats,
lifelines, on the table of our first writing seminar,
nascent writers, crewmates in this literary port.
Walking about the deck, learning starboard from port,
hoping the seaworthy glossary would pull me
like Polaris towards true north, towards truth, and still
I plundered worn-out metaphors from old mythologies,
the Greeks' and mine, until the captain,
really, the director of our program, begged me to stop,
disembark
find a bar
drink ouzo with Greek sailors,
smell fragrances of fennel, aniseed, and hazelnut,
watch any visage that had wrinkled into story,
remove all vessels that had Grecian bows and sterns
relinquish Homer and Eurydice and Neptune
replace sea metaphors with ones
that opened up the ocean's floor
and all that I would dredge in all the days
and weeks and months and lives ahead,
the conversations to be held with as-yet-
unknown friends and lovers, in places close
as coffee shops and bars that lined the
port in Baltimore I would call home, so far

away from all the fictions myth had given me,
so close to what I'd salvage as my truth.

2017

Spring Catalog

From J. Peterman's catalog. "Clearly, people want things
that make their lives the way they wish they were."

Long Sleeve 1947 Dress

Thought to be "the" dress that let the female form sashay,
I always think, on me the dress will not remove my doubts about
my style,
nor add a Hollywood-like luster to my life, but still I manage to
dog-ear the page
and hope that *artful emphasis on legs, hips, waist, and bust*
begins to draw me as I'd like to see myself.

Some Innocent Embellishment

an off-the-shoulder dress, one that I dream of dancing in,
my shoulder, not the dress, the lure for you,
someone I've thought so much about
that marginalia in my journals are scripted with your name.

Dots

vintage shouts the polka-dotted dress, one I'll wear when speaking
to a group that hangs on every syllable I utter,
one you conjure up, just as you consider whom to ask about
the weather,
what to choose for dinner, or whom you'll sit beside at your
next meeting,
all you'll see is me.

Pleat de Resistance

The catalog shows wide-leg pants that Hepburn must have worn
while leaving work for after-hours cocktails.
I see myself join her and others for a Gibson,

confident my pleated wide-legged chiffon pants
reveal me as I want to be received, uncloaking only
who I want to show, and surely not who I am.

2017

Palimpsest

So thin this paper you have chosen for your words,
so thin, this membrane-like translucence
wearing well the scratching of your pen,
the laying over, reinscribing, overwriting
ink that sinks into the parchment of
others' words seeped like yours,
extracted from life's exchanges,
from conversations, contracts, vows,
a diary of truths of who you
thought you were. Sometimes your pen's a scribe,
copying another's hand to practice yours;
sometimes you only watch how vellum
soaks up ink, the letters drying
as you wait for postscripts. Is what we
write a copy of what was there before,
the *scripto inferior*, the underwriting that someone long ago
had penned, papyrus where so many
lists and letters and lessons lived,
before all were scraped away,
reminding us writing can begin
again the very thoughts someone might have had before,
scrubbing clean the worn, the trite,
the overused, a calligraphy you know is yours, for now.

2017 ~ Published in OASIS JOURNAL 2018 Anthology

Moth Orchid

That day you'd brought me the moth orchid
its blossoms blocked your head, you holding beauty at my door,
I thought not
how lovely, how telling, how wordlessly you offered love
but pictured word games, the ones where we would change
or rearrange the letters in a word of four
to form one new. Now phalaenopsis, or phal, the orchid's name,
I changed from moth to mote to mite to mine to mind
and then, as you continued not to speak, I heard
the word games that we'd played when questions
of what love meant, what two could be,
what caring asked of those who did, or could not.

The moth orchid stayed with me for months, its blooms
remained as long, and you,
the disappearing benefactor
had helped me stretch my word game, changing your excuse
that sadly had become excise, the orchid opened up for me to
orchard.

2017 ~ Published in 300 Days of Sun, Volume 2, Issue 1, Spring 2019

This is a test.
This station is conducting a test of the
Emergency Broadcasting System.
This is only a test.

Only a test   not its opposite
which would be
not a test but the real thing?

the old Philco in the corner of the living room seemed real,
pulled me, a 50s child, into hypnotic visuals,
swept me into its green screen opening
black and white Clarabells and Captain Kangaroos
asking, testing me,
remember my rhymes and measure my manners.

only a test   not its opposite
would that be
not the blue book but the dry run?

I have heard in repeated short staccato phrases
all I remember of my echoed past,
mistakes repeated, then hidden,
failed tests in relationships, in friendships, in me.

I hear the raven this morning,
in the parking lot where two ravens live,
moving from lamppost to roof,
from edges to corners, their gurgling their soundings
deeply from their throats. I'm held by the sounds,

twined with wire, twirled from my car, torqued to listen
to the second-long knocking noises, alerted to a possibility
of danger, waiting for the ending note, a beak's snapping
tapping into my remembering the sounds of breakage, of endings,
divorcing happiness from my life, embracing feathers to fly to
new moments.

only a test   not its opposite
even the ravens warn
and wait, is this a test?

Waiting for "And that's the way it is" in the 60s, waiting
for another day that tested who we were, who we
could be, but left alone inside our homes, our cubby holes,
sitting atop our own lampposts, did we wonder if it was all
a test, or was it really happening

CubanMissileCrisisJFKdeadCivilRightsmarchesVietnam
JFK deadMLK
deadRFKArmstrongAldrinfootstepsonthemoons-
mall stepsformanonegiantleapformankind

Fastforwardtotheimagesweseealongwithwhatweknowasviraltruth
Acrownwithspikessurroundingvirionitstwistedgenescommanding
Usinvadingusinternallyandchangingtheworldoutsideforever.

and how did we learn what we had learned when
we kept hearing the warning sounds, the raven's calls,
the Emergency Broadcast System in all of us
silently signaling all of us
this is not a test
this is my life and our lives
this is your turn to prep

to do a trial run to learn what the exam will ask of you,
your actions the way
that you become the *testum:*
you, the earthen pot that centuries ago assayed precious
metals, you, collecting what you need to assay the truth.

No.

This is no longer a test.
This is not even a warning signal.
This is real. Listen.

*2018 ~ Published in Capsule Stories 2021, The End Will Not
Be Sugared*

Wandering with Magritte

Today's a day for wandering with Magritte,
for keeping pace with floating bowler hats
and canvases concealing while revealing
what lies just beyond the window's glass.
Those many windows tease us,
frame the problem of seeking
what lies beyond the pane, behind the shutter,
wanting the green-fringed tree much more
than what we see upon the easel. Who's to say
if that green apple could consume a face, or
if there was a face behind it anyway? Or if
the trunk's segmented self contained
another home, or just some cells? Or if, indeed,
the photo that I carry will always
have you holding poppies and the one you say
you have of me will fill my silhouette with clouds and stars.
We promenade back where we began; paintings
whisper what they mean. We catch Magritte,
open up the windows.

2018

Ghosting

All I see are ghosts—white shuddering wisps
outlining all the images from seven weeks in Poland—
already family there seems ghost-like,
so far removed so far away.
I, home, emotionally downloading
pictures where my tears bestow
a graininess to everyone and everything in Warsaw.
So, I think I'm seeing ghosts.
We're well aware how much like apparitions we become,
a contrail of wordless skies,
evaporating touch, but, if we're lucky,
pictures clearly show family's always here
even when we feel like ghosts.

2018

My Bedroom and Van Gogh's

The third version, identifiable by its smaller size, is equally
autobiographical. Both exhibit a nervous energy and sense of
incompletion so unlike the restful respite of the first.
~ Mary Tompkins Lewis about Van Gogh's
paintings of his bedrooms

It had been Papa's room, wallpapered in pigeon-feather tones, a
room my mom had cordoned off after my grandpa died; the room
he slept in on the second floor, died in, the room our mother
honored by locking it, preserving it, keeping me and my brother
out. Old world custom, respect, depression?

I never knew. Our patriarch, our Russian grandfather, a tailor,
my mother's father, the tall thin immigrant who sewed into his
children's future all the hopes that this new world might hold, had
lived in what we'd called our Papa's room. I don't remember much
about it 'til I'd grown beyond my small bedroom chamber on the
second floor, was told that I could have my Papa's bedroom when
I reached ten. And so my girlhood dreams began in that unlocked
bedroom now dipped in pink: pink walls, pink windowsills, pink
curtains, pink friezes of pale cherubim, pink scatter rugs. A room
of ballet dreams, old diaries, chenille bedspread with its patterned
fleur-de-lis beckoning Versaille to come to Boston. One bureau
drawer still had Papa's thimbles, spectacles, the small bell that
customers had rung to summon him from the back room of his
shop, where he repaired to sew and stitch and mend. This is where
I listened to top 40 songs on Saturdays and first saw drops of blood
that said I'd come of age. This is where I lived with other "little
women"—Jo and Meg, Amy and Beth had shared what family
life I'd hoped I'd had. This is where I'd typed so many poems that
helped me live through my Dad's telling me he was leaving all of us,
where I overheard my mother tell a friend (words lifting through

the spaces that old doorways' frames will leave) she'd found a lump. In the heavy air of humid summers, where even maple trees could muster up no breeze, I'd lie upon that chenille bedspread thinking, when all seemed lost, I might be able to call to Papa, reach him like the ring bell had so many years ago, to stitch him to my life, create a pattern I could alter.

2018 ~ Published in OASIS JOURNAL 2018

Apparently

You had another family, other daughters, sons, and even
wife, you had another home you'd take the streetcar and the bus to
even though we promised we would pick you up in
Kenmore Square.
Each night you said you'd try to get to Little League, to dinner,
home to
us. Apparently we waited up and then, when we had gone to
bed, just
as we fell asleep, we'd hear the front door open, the loudening
of voices,
the whispering of Mom's, the sounds of footsteps coming up
the stairs,
our feigning sleep if Mom looked in our rooms. Apparently
next days
were always quieter, you not there, you'd left again and slowly
took the little that you had at home to where apparently you really
lived. Apparently the story that we heard was that you
hadn't 'signed
on' to be with us, as husband or as dad, and what apparently we
did was
sign you out.

2019

Was Autumn Always My Antidote to Summer?

I

more vespers,
less sun,
more moon,
our conversations, connections, readings,
for soothing, not solutions.

II

New shoes,
slippery soles we'd scrape to school
until the sheen wore off,
Mom's message from home:
make sure you don't slip up.

III

Sweet cherries, *cerises douces,*
French syllables just as sweet,
let the mouth linger, ours hovering
as we bit Bing orbs, probing for the pits,
the end of
Wenatchee's best cherries,
its orchards a half mile closer to the moon.

IV

Old photographs, figuring why we took them,
Smith & Butler's antique doorknobs
storefront display that autumn day
as maple leaves did move,
and I still cast a shadow in that bronzing world.

V

You're standing near the art, the mounted *Summer Bloom*
a whorl of resin, holding seeds and pods and birds' nests
while all the stem fingers move around like clock hands,
more organic than the nine to five I'm used to,
a way that helps me move into your newest season.

VI

That fall I moved into a larger room, and
missed
the little room that had been mine since birth,
adjacent to the attic, room with two doors,
room with a staircase, several ways to go.
That fall I moved into a room with trees
outside
and learned to feel the seasons,
smell them, understand the ways we both come and go.

2019 – Published in Capsule Stories, Autumn 2020 Edition

The Last Word(s)

Lately been thinking of last words, mortality on the mind,
pandemic's presence infiltrating moments, movement,
musings that this might be among my last moments,
so much so that sheltering in place seems to open, not
shut, the search for more, not more in the sense of more paths,
more in the way of what matters, who matters,
sends me back to correspondence collected in shipping boxes
reminding me of so many places I'd been, so much dust
surrounding all that's been saved, formerly savored notes
and cards I'd saved for rainy days, so thank you, pandemic,
for the ultimate
rainy day, for opening me up to reading words sent to me
when dialogue with "others" has temporarily disappeared,
thinking where my words have ended up, in others' musty
memories.
And what words would it be that I'd utter last, my fascination
with last words growing as quickly as reported COVID-19 cases,
Oh wow
Steve Jobs' last syllables express the precipice
I imagine I might hope to see. My postcard phonics sent home
declaring *great time at the top of* or *can't believe I'm here outside of*
shared with those at home, saying so much and little all at once.
And now, at home (it seems, eternally),
I've had time to wonder what my message
might be if I grow nearer to last words,
that maybe no one had ever known me
as little as I have myself, that maybe no words
will be enough.

2019 ~ Published in Capsule Stories, Isolation Edition 2020

Rent for our Room on Earth

(from Muhammed Ali)

Not sure where that is, sometimes, my room, my home,
but this West Coast city has too many zip codes,
and too many faces that turn away
don't look at you, sometimes beyond, afraid connecting
might mean
you want something and here there are too many
whose wants aren't being met
whose needs go unwatched whose backs we don't have.
Sounds on this hot Sunday rise like hot air sending gospel notes
beyond the outdoors stage, lifting words that catch up with my feet
so I am walking keeping time
walking and watching and walking and listening and walking
and hearing
"Give me your arms for the broken hearted" and San Jose cried with
Dayton and El Paso and Gilroy.
"Give me your heart for the ones forgotten" and San Jose cries for all
who don't have refuge.
"Give me your eyes so I can see" and I cry until my tears clear my
eyes, and I hear
the words on your t-shirt sing to me of Ali, you walking towards
me, me looking at you with you.
Service to others is the rent you pay for your room here on Earth
My room here on Earth—so many rooms where I've slept and risen
loved, been lost, saved, often still looking for redemption, my
many lives
spent trying to understand words we wear, words we feel, words
I say.

I stop to mouth the words to you, to all of you, that yes I'll have
your back
I'll read and listen and watch and hear and see and see and see.

2019 ~ Published online in TheNewVerse.News September 15 2019

Their Mark, Their Way

You are designing yourself,
your arms thin columns inked
with indigo, a winged *lilitu* I think
you said, or *kinnara*, hybrid human
forms fitting you,
growing towards you,
flying with you from where you've been,
the young woman I taught years ago,
a poet sharing what she shed.
Today at lunch
we still are teacher/student, not sure which
I am now, but sure that you are both
the seeker and the answer, a balance that
I find pronounced in Borneo as *Mahatala*,
West Africa as *Nana Bulukul*, and you,
dear being, you pronounce yourself
with dermis covered with these footnotes
helping the revealing of evolving stories,
like the hair that's now appearing on your chest.
You tell me I'd inspired one tattoo, a wall
of stones that covers one forearm, because
I'd told you long ago before you could break
through, you'd need to know the rubble
in the building, what to keep and what to
throw, and then you'd find the stones
no longer walls, but rooms, and rooms
no longer lonely, but
connected to a home.

2019 ~ Published in Hamline LitLink 2019, and Soul Lit 2019

Weeding

These days it takes more than trowels to tame the weeds,
days, in fact, of sifting through the lists of plants pretending
to be lawn. I've read these masqueraders' names, magnifi-
cent sounds
that stop my hand and spade, pause, ask
why would I remove purslane, poor weed, not bad,
just 'misunderstood' the gardeners' dictionary says.
And so with creeping sorrel, thistle, lambsquarters, my
list grows long, my hand grows still, my task grows harder
than a simple yank or pull.
Maybe these weeds, like I have been, are simply misperceived,
can offer color, texture, more than ornamental fringe, by some
considered even good enough to eat. I wonder if they know they
are impostors, a syndrome where I've roots,
feeling not quite green enough when blades must be virescent,
too unseasoned to be seen as sage.
And while I do remove some dandelions, deep roots beneath
the lawn so many feet, I take their puffball heads
blow the seeds remembering
how I held their flowers long ago,
when they, to me, were flowers, without pretense,
and I was who I am, without disguise.

2019 ~ Published Issue 2: In Flore, Second Chance Lit

Ice Skating Scene, Viewed from San Jose Museum of Art

Not even close to Avercamp's frozen canal, this
scene from my museum perch, me with my coffee,
cream drizzled over its surface, thoughts warmed while
watching this California ice rink just outside:
a girl leaping on her skates, a couple holding on for balance
and for love, a youthful game of tag on ice. No flourishes,
no horse-drawn sleds nor sheaths of wheat nor holes being cut
for fishing.
The skaters move, always clockwise, always leaning
forward into their next crossovers, their next jumps,
sensing bordering
boards, edging grapevines. It's not too far a jump for me
skating backwards to Massachusetts,
to frozen ponds where muffled,
mittened, bundled up, skates ready, I'd join the skaters.
The best would twirl and twizzle on their own,
the jocks would wield their sticks and pucks.
The rest of us, we'd look for leaders, someone who'd form a whip.
We'd search for hands to clasp, then forming frozen bonds
we'd serpentine our way across the ice,
avoiding cattails poking, peeking through the edges' cracks,
hoping not to find we'd lost the line,
hoping not to be peripheral prisoners.
Those were moments
of both fear and pleasure, moments I've relived on many
other canvases,
the fear of losing someone's grip while yearning to let go, the
pleasure of letting go while

fearing what alone might mean. For now, my coffee soothes, the
rink remains both
outdoors and within,
as I remember what it took to warm my frozen feet and heart
when I went skating on and then beyond the pond.

2019

Gumlines, among others

Build-up, they call it, the slow accretion colorless
at first. Later I guess you'd think my teeth had bathed
in egg yolk if I'd let it go that far. Especially if I were smiling today.
But today, I'm not thinking recession as in my gums, but as in
our economy, how the graphs display the Vs that look like troughs
not mountains. Feels too much like my slackline has no anchors,
that I'll be eternally between, above, not able to begin or
end. Reminds
me of those hemlines we called handkerchief, the 70s loved them, I
loved them, made me feel that I was whirling standing still.
More standing
still on stars or footprints or just blue tape lined up outside Target
or the post office, I'm wondering if last night's dreams are
still available,
shelved someplace, line forming here, I'd even pay for their
retrieval. Lost
moments, lines breaking up. I'm back inside my mouth, imagining
what they'll
find after I'm beyond words. Not anything as artful as the lazurine
the 1,000-year-old teeth held, medieval teeth, medieval scribe,
medieval woman
breathing in the bright blue pigment, licking her brush while
blue began
its residence in her mouth. What would be found—a piece of
jasmine rice,
the inhalation of surprise and joy, the drupelets of a final rasp-
berry, the
exhalation of all the lines I'd thought about and hadn't had a chance
to write.

2020 - Published May 19, 2020, TheNewVerse.News

A Memory of Winter, Denver

Later, I would describe our time as colorless,
winter had taken care of that, whiteness over all,
your apartment gleamed modern, silver, Scandi,
tubular arrangements holding all you owned
together. A few times we tried the trails around
the campus where you taught, our herringboned
tracks revealing how unsteady we were.
Later, driving to the airport, winter
pelting us with sleet, the wipers froze,
clock hands to the hour two, mocking us, our
mittened cleaning of the windshield
only cleared one side.
A colorless goodbye, the blandest promises
to stay in touch, a mutual relief in boarding, leaving.
Far below, a winter without powder had gone
straight to ice.

2020 ~ Published in Capsule Stories, Winter 2020 Edition

Piscean Fate

Reliably there, two columns near the comics,
sometimes, Sundays, nestled near the puzzle,
my daily horoscope, the go-to for my questions then,
a child yearning for quick-takes,
fast answers, book flap summaries for my life. Now,
much older, still reading daily, weekly, monthly,
more wry smiles, more knowing disappointments, absorbing
universal conditionals for every sign, the *"fun"*
appearing for my Pisces forecast echoed for my Aries
neighbor, the *"balance"* that will come
when stress abates, resides with Taurus, too.
Imagining the horoscope a forecast, I must
have used the words as breadcrumbs leading
me to come, to go, to join, to leave, depending
on the astral prophecy. An easy conversation meant
Mercury had messaged me and all was well.
Now I use the daily signs not as predictors for my path
but notes that all twelve divinations, blessed
by stars and planets, cross all skies with life's
emotional accessories. We find ourselves alike in what
our journeys might become, and like the star kit I once
bought to put the Milky Way above my young son's head,
his ceiling lighted long after lights went out, I find I
look at Pisces just to see what stars might strew along my path,
but also know the comfort of the sky when all is dark and quiet
with the stars peeled off.

2020

Rehearsal: Running Lines

What did you see?

It's our first run-through, you helping me run lines.
It's this one that's stopped me. You ask me to move
words in my mouth, syllable by syllable, as if they
had un-partnered lives, far from other plosives.
My mouth is now flask for sounds
moves me from meaning towards memory.

What

Am I asking about the world's indefiniteness,
whispering or wailing about the image you will
or did not share with me, the one I need (-ed) to make
sense of you, and me, and it.

Did

It's the past tense I shuffle,
past to past perfect back to present,
shifting vision to what had appeared,
opening my eyes to what's been straight ahead.

You

In the familiar or formal, in the accusatory or beseeching,
it's always been you, that other whose help
or hindrance led me to this conversation, my
questions always start with arrows and
boomerang back, but not to me.

See

At best, my eyes stay on the image:
the old woman, shawl enveloped,
until I only see the slope and shape
of the much younger woman,

scarf flying behind her hair. So,
when I say 'see' I'm really mouthing silently
look more.
When we run lines again maybe
I'll know inflection links to truth
and sometimes even get there.

2020

Trepanation

For a large part of human prehistory, people around the
world practiced trepanation: a crude surgical procedure...
involving forming a hole in the skull of a living person
by...drilling, cutting, or scraping ...Shiva, the Hindu
god of altered consciousness, was trepanned.

The openings in these skulls,
               discovered, recovered in southern Russia's fields,
round elliptical holes, each
possibly releasing pain, or
perhaps inviting spirits ways in or out of
               two men, two women, and young girl's beings,
the point of entry, obelion, sounds more and more
like oblivion to me, as I touch the top of my head,
imagining a tunnel to clear thinking, or would it
be more pain, more acumen, and maybe, with luck,
less absurdity.
Could I imagine letting light in
while letting devils out,
my mind tripping over itself,
my neurons stumbling,
crossed wires obliterated for the sake of clarity,
my instincts say let there be chaos,
let creativity be spawned. That's what
Amanda Feilding did, drill her skull,
felt the hole let tides come in, saw her dreams
taper off to calm. If I could, I'd open
up my skull to let the demons out, the
shrapnel of old arguments, the weaponry
of misunderstandings, nightmares of
all bitter moments never able to bring
sweet learning ones. Lightened, lighted,

I imagine trepanning myself, and,
in the small space of the o-shape
forming concentric circles in my thoughts, I
re-imagine me, broken open, whole again.

2020

Unfinished: Thoughts Left Visible

From the exhibit at The Met Breuer Museum of Art, May 2016

The lure of the unfinished, uneven canvas ever waiting for its pigments,
Turner's waves, or are they skies, that fall? Disassembled hands
attached to no one, their sculptor long gone and languishing. Their
palms cupped, praying for corporal extension in this *non finito* moment
where they await arms and torsos.

From room to room, I fantasize faces not filled in, skies that burst
with blue in parts of Auver-sur-Oise, the tendrils of a maiden's hair
da Vinci hinted at. James Hunter, black draftee, his name stays
with me,
sat for his portrait only once before Vietnam called, and here all
that's left
a face waiting for a body.

We have these rooms, we do, attended by the guardians of the self
who keep
unfinished moments ready for when we stop and put on the face we
never showed.
It's not too late to finish what we decide to sketch,
what we've learned we can become,
to fend off those who never asked us what our hours were,
where we'd left our paints.

2020

Journeying

After Gayle Kaune's *A Story About the Journey*

I am that bunker defending my life,
the body hidden on the dumbwaiter,
the unsolved in a series of murders.

One day I touched the big eyes
of the sad-eyed girl staring at me, her portrait
Keane had painted, hanging outside my aunt's room
those silent days of eavesdropping outside that room
picking words like lint from conversations
scrubbing meaning mounded like laundry waiting
to be washed. The summer of feeling sad-eyed always,
the summer of sickness, the summer of my mother's cancer.

A summer about my heart, the one I felt
perforated from so many woundings,
today, displayed as the heart-shaped
ruby paperweight covering my mother's
sepia photo, she young and well, and
covered by crimson hues of health.

I want to read old postcards
plucked from bookshops' bins,
quotes from Milton, Chaucer, Voltaire
streaming sense into my skin, like *Solitude sometimes
is best society.* I tuck them in my purse,
hopeful amulets.

Once I went to MOMA SF to wallow in
Warhol, liked Marilyn with blue skin,

knew why the soup cans found him.

Memory is like that, like the finale
leaving the viewers wondering if there'll
be a sequel, like the last time we slept
together, you'd figured out the end,
I'd only hoped for more.

2020

Puzzled and Puzzling

It's Sunday and I'm driving to church for the early service. My traditionalist husband won't come any more to this very liberal Episcopal community. Where is there real discourse, he wonders. I've got NPR on, and the timing's perfect—I can listen to Will Shortz's puzzle and catch the next week's puzzler before I have to head into church. *What country, if you remove its last letter, also leaves a native?* Inside, I pick up this Sunday's Service Bulletin, our guide to the readings and order of the service, say hello to this week's church greeters—she is always smiling and he always asks whether my husband is coming back soon—and I keep thinking of the Will Shortz puzzle. I need to don white robes, to 'vest,' as I serve as Lay Eucharistic Minister and will offer, later, Prayers for the People. I review the names parishioners have left in the Prayer Book so I won't stumble during service, still thinking of that puzzle as I do during moments for standing, for kneeling, for my offering the chalice as the *blood of Christ, the cup of salvation,* for my wondering over the entire act of transubstantiation even while I'm offering Christ's blood to those at the altar rail (I've chosen to simply receive a blessing—and have not sipped from the cup for a while—first because of flu season and now the *coronavirus,* but partly, to be honest, because I'm still puzzling over this part of the service, one I accept as miracle, but one that eludes me, and only sometimes offers comfort.) In his most jocular and authentic tone, our Rector reminds us we're all here as Christ for each other until we find our, as he puts it, "dirt bed" and hopefully (as I persuade myself) ascend somewhere somehow. I'm puzzled by my son's problems that I cannot solve; I put him and his family on our prayer list, but then, too, these are prayers offered sometimes, like wishes, unable to be granted. Shall I go over to visit my son in Warsaw for longer than usual—maybe six weeks this time—to help them out, me, his mother bearing a chalice of compassion, hoping to offer salve and prayer if not solution. I recess with the others at the service's closing, recess, and finally figure out one puzzle.

Puzzle not too hard
German, Swede, Somali
Heart without 't' lets me listen fully

2020 ~ Published in Soul-Lit 2020

A Perennial, This Annual

This annual requires more than showing up, preliminary questions
scaled from 1 - 5, continua of *always, sometimes,* and then *not at all,*
exploring what my aging body's come to be.

Whether I can see or not, can stand or kneel, can simply be,
the inquiries demand I look more deeply into functioning, with questions
for the parts of me denying that I'm aging, but all

reminding me that this, the specimen I have become, can
be evaluated,
all by numbers, reducing mind and body to become
the total of this annual interrogation, a sum of questions

answered well enough, illuminating some of what I am, now
many decades old, or what I dread might have become, assumes
I have no further questions, at my age, or maybe ones that I've forgotten now.

2020

Mom's Box Grater

After she died, I wanted, more than the cameo brooch she'd pin
to every lapel, her box grater, that precursor, of sorts,
of all food processors, the rectangular metal box that shared
four different ways of slicing up the world. Her deeply veined
hands would set the grater on the kitchen table, waxed paper spread
to catch the shredded, sliced, slivered pieces of whatever foods
had needed whittling down. Carrots disappeared before my eyes,
returning when the grater lifted, curled adornments for a salad,
stewing vegetables for the brisket mother'd boil until it fell apart.
Even with a size that never spoke of domination among the
kitchen tools,
the box grater was what I'd been wary of. I'd seen my mother's
fingers bruised after a bout with it, entering the ring of preparation,
anticipating minor wounds. It was a tool I'd graduate to, fluent
in its metalled Braille, knowing which opening—oval, half-moon, plank—
translated best the food to recipe. My first abraded fingers felt
as if I'd been awarded medals, understanding that my
taming foods was one of many ways Mom was preparing me
for life, fingers raw and chafed that still presented a full hand.

2020 ~ Your Daily Poem, November 2021

If seeing makes it so,

My eyes would squint the lilac bush into color, if they could,
as if the possibility of fragranced white clusters might blossom
just because of will. Outside my patio, the woody shrub bears
no resemblance to itself in spring, just twiggy arteries with promises
of blooms. No drift of perfumed petals, no petalled carpet
to my door: only bumps on branches whisper to my eyes
their future flowers.

The aftermath of lilacs blooming, the sweet brevity of color
taken in and stored, reminders that our moments are not long,
but still intense enough to press between two pages,
bloom or photograph, a saving, an inhalation of time shared,
remembered whichever presence is preserved, when lilac
season is long gone, as long as we can focus on
what we had taken time to see, if only in that moment.

2020

The Great Conjunction

Bundled up and with binoculars, we are contemporary
versions of Ptolemy and Aglaonice,
standing on our driveway, necks tilted back, our bodies a bipod
for our binoculars, finding the yellowish crescent of
December's moon,
and what we think might be the great conjunction of Jupiter
and Saturn.
Maybe it's because we often are not part of something bigger than
ourselves, because we've missed the comet tails and then eclipses,
not standing in the hemisphere that's best for viewing,
we've kept our celestial appointment, keeping company with
Genghis Khan
800 years ago, who also watched this joining in the skies.
There are, of course, glow-in-the-dark star stickers we'd placed
on our son's ceiling when he was so little that he'd thought
the sky had entered to illuminate his bedtime. And, then there are
the many other simultaneous occurrences that are joinings:
the House and Senate, the King and Queen, the lords and ladies,
the earth and sea, the heavens and Earth, the living and the dead,
the unspoken and the thought, the unsaid and the truth,
the haves and the have-nots, the remembered, the forgotten,
until we hear, you and me, from friends that what we thought
we'd seen could not have been both Jupiter and Saturn, but only
one of them, given where we live. So, you and I, conjoined now
for some years, made a decision, decided that our eyes
had seen the great conjunction, and like the Christmas Star,
we would believe in something larger than ourselves, needing to
in times when either/or has reigned too long.
Like all good conjunctions, this conjoining, not choosing one
or other,

a great conjunction, Jupiter and Saturn.
is how we'll complete this 2020 year, allusion always
to a greater sight, now helping us see a new night sky.

2020 – Published in NewVerse News 2020

Quiz Night

There's never time enough to prep
for game night, a quiz bowl tasking us to recall
shreds of what we may have learned in school, or
on the fly, in weekly summaries of news, or headlines
caught on screens when we are scrolling for something else.
And as the rounds go on, we learn
what now remains and what has left us: bits and pieces
fastening the world's so many facts into one bowl
of questions. Stumbling through the sequence theme,
remembering that Conrad followed Aldrin as a lunar walker,
forgetting when we celebrate so many days,
lucidly recalling Star Wars Day with glee, going forth
to flounder with the word describing
groups of cats, then pouncing on the answer to
trick questions like the day New Zealanders would
honor Christmas, we slowly, laughingly, emerge
now laden with new trivia, which slowly, quietly,
too, will disappear. It's in the hours following quiz night
I most remember details of my life, the ones I've
shelved, then lost, then scrounge around for,
the names of friends who let me cry about lost
parents, breakups, the help a poem gave me
when I was down, the bad hair days that
I recall with smiles (the purple streak supposed to be
a flower in my hair, too often thought to be
a mid-life crisis.)
It's in the days that follow
quiz night I begin to put together my own questions,
ones I often ask myself, and answer differently depending
on the day and time—like who I am if I would take off all

the masks I wear, or what it is I'm holding onto,
and mostly, asking me who I am today?

2021

Magical Realism

Inspired by art of Christopher Whitney

Both are miracles.
One seduces by illusion, the other tempts
the eyes to squint the distant shape into a bird.
I've wanted my own heaviness to lift itself into a breeze,
grind down the coarseness of old memories and conversations
into polished stones, easier to balance, kinder to my heart.
The possibility of flight has kept my vision on alert for moments to
ascend, to leave the quartz and mica, the granite claims that hold us
to the earth. Black bird. Rock pile. Both picture balance and escape,
the fragile tension between what's near and what might fly away.

2020-21

Escape Plans

Inspired by Banksy's latest installation art on
the walls of Reading Gaol in England

We do it without thinking, sighting those red block letters,
EXIT
reassuring our leaving places where we've found ourselves,
or more precisely, where we've found ourselves lost,
in theaters, malls, relationships,
those gathering spaces where,
not sure sometimes why we're there,
we fold away small notes to self, including routes by which
we'll leave.
It's been a year since we took leave
from what? Routines, connections, worn-out paths of
customary comings, anticipated goings,
a year of changing patterns, forswearing the habitual,
creating novel ways to meet, to share, to love, to spend
time trying not to think where we should have been,
envisioning new plans to leave the here and now
without abandoning ourselves. What's left
when signs are not available? The word itself lies next to
others in the dictionary, including existential, and they
become new guides for taking leave, and flight, and hold
of who we are
as we discover what
it is to paint our own way out of boxes, out of corners,
over all walls that restrict our freedoms
finding what we've missed seeing.

2021 ~ Published Spring 2021 in NewVerse News

Take away the accoutrements,
get to the essence.
~ from Anna Halprin, dancer/choreographer

In this picture you're barefoot on your deck,
a wooden acre wrapped around your home,
your natural dance studio, where cloud and sky and sun and blue
help bodies become dancers, where singular experiences
beyond the body find their way inside,
becoming gesture, movement, giving answers
to why we move this way, not that, into, around,
under the others on the deck, the patterns of their limbs
and feet and hands letting story enter the body, exit as dance.

You teach by showing that you move for love, to share
what lives inside your heart so others find what lives in theirs.
You write that when you eat a carrot
you eat the sun, that we are but the human dance
of life, recycling everything we see and touch and feel
into the you and you and you we brush past
on this deck, beyond this deck, into the trees, into
the ecstasy of branches reaching.
                                         I watch you move
others to move themselves to be more, feel more,
uncover ways we can connect, to treat
the very ground we stand upon as holy, the feet that
touch it then and now and hence as sacred, the hands
that reach above our heads potential wings that soar,
that share, that speak the only message that will matter,
that we all have mattered here.

2021 ~ Published in NewVerse News June 2021

A few of Judy Chicago's favorite things

[inspired by a photo memoir in the
Wall Street Journal Magazine, 2020]

That an airbrush is in the picture surprises me
as does the photo of Anais Nin,
the former what helped Chicago's artistry,
the latter, a reminder women serve
as muses for each other. My eyes stop on the
poster she named "Stranded," unable to discern
exactly what I'm seeing, but drawn to what she called
the series that it's from, *The End:*
A Meditation on Death and Extinction. I am
aware the floor is set with items that she loves,
reminds me that she'd set a larger table, one
for women, where she gathered 39 to honor,
including oh so many who'd not been on
invitation lists before—women, artists,
ones deserving of a place to sit. My favorite
item, though, of hers is accidental, maybe.
Fastened to the window a wrought iron curly cue
casts shadows on the studio floor, will disappear
by sunset. All women looking at what Judy's made
know we won't.

2021
Short-listed for Oprelle Publications 2021 "Matter" Poetry Contest

How to Make a Fortune Cookie
and maybe understand the fortune

It would be easy, wouldn't it,
if all we had to do was measure out and cut
the strips for all our maybes, then write
what we predict or hope or fear will happen,
put them aside, which sometimes we can do
with thoughts pre-occupying us, then go
preheat the oven,
beat egg white, flour, sugar, salt,
add almond flavoring and oil, then stir
until the thickened batter can be spooned
upon the baking sheet. Wait fifteen minutes,
remove the baked dough circlets, place
one strip of what the future holds on each,
and fold in half.

Come back later, break
open one or all of these small fortune
pastries, lifting out the paper from its womb, birthing
gently what you either hope or dread will be the words
pronouncing future themes, hopes, riddles, ironies,
the stuff of fortune cookies and of life. You've barely tasted
what that future is, and start, in bites
to realize how you hold
what it will take to feast upon it.

Soul-Lit, Spring 2022

Hide, Don't Seek

was not, you know, the game's real name,
the one I'd plead to serve as hider, already
knowing how alone I'd feel as seeker, counting
to one hundred, abandoned by the hiders,
finding the world as silent as the tree I leaned against,
eyes shut,
my world bereft of shrieks and giggling, of any and all
movements. Quiet.

I've changed the game's name as I'm remembering
you, my father, you'd said you'd be at home by 6, or at
recitals no later than the curtains being drawn, or at
my birthday parties, helping with the games, or at
the hospital when I'd come down, ironically, with echo virus,
my stomach pain calling out to you to come to see me.

I think I had stopped counting
both the numbers and on you,
when hide, don't seek, became the new name of the game
you played with us, the family you
left behind to count while at the maple tree,
the baseball field, the kitchen table,
attic, cellar, backyard,
anywhere we were
you weren't.

I counted on that all my childhood,
sadly, took that game with me
when seeking men
I'd hoped would replace you.

Most knew only rules for hide, don't seek,
and not the rules where it felt
safe to be a seeker, as well as
to be sought and found.

Soul-Lit, Spring 2022

Compos[t]ing Myself

I remember times when soil smelled rich,
a kind of coffee-bean rich, a kind
of patchouli rich, a rich scenting flaring my nostrils,
inhaling more.
The time we worked our garden soil
composting it, the elements of peat and perlite
caking fingernails, our prepping
beds for rows and rows of plants
yearning for elements beyond clay. We dreamt
of growing foxglove, ferns and fuchsias,
entwining them with flowers mixing other letters
into soil with pansies, daffodils, impatiens.
But it was always soil, prepared, that led to color,
soil inhabiting our very blood and bones,
a deep affinity for dust to dust we have within,
rich dark coffee-colored soil, aromas lifting up and
taking us to early earth when scientists say the smell
was more like rotten eggs, rich with H2S. This richness lives
within me, my body's future with the possibility of
decomposing into one cubic yard of soil,
along with wood, alfalfa, even straw, all
assisting me along the way to my new form,
my inert self reduced to fragrant future supplements
for growing flowers after I have gone.

Something to think about, while legislators ponder laws
to handle soil that's human-sourced. Right now, it's not
Assembly Bill 501 I'm thinking of; I'm smelling soil, the
rich soil that flowers hunger for, the soil that's fed
my soul, the gardening days when turning over dirt

was very much like leafing through a sacred text,
when I've translated who I've been
into the earth from which I've come.

September 2021, NewVerse News
Spring 2022, Soul-Lit

Practicing Lectio Divina

It's gone beyond Bible reading, beyond
the invitation to
read more deeply
spiraling from my head into my heart,
and maybe even to my soul,
beyond re-readings of that psalm,
the one announcing plenty
when all I'd felt was pain.
Silencio. Becoming quiet always
a challenge, how to stop syllables
from streaming, from emergence
into sounds I might regret.
Lectio. Reading out loud helps
letters seen through tears
stop moving, sorts them into
words, then feelings, then
something I'll remember when
we're done, when you're gone.
Meditatio. The sitting, the re-reading,
the watching of the scenes where you'd
inhabited my life. What do I want
to remember? Need to forget?
Oratio. Not that I've not thought
of prayer, but what I'm seeing,
listening to, re-living, doesn't seem
to fit what supplication asks. Not
sure my prayer's ready, but I'll
remember all the letters, words,
all letters, all that has been communicated
well, and not.

Contemplatio. Rest, lie down, remember,
recline, re-enter, restore, renew·
your life with words that heal, and
leave behind the ones that hurt, trusting
you can return to this again, this you
you have become, reading more closely
clearly cleanly than you've ever done before,
you're closely reading sacred text, now,
when you learn more of what you've meant.

2021

CHYRON

~electronically generated captions superimposed on screens

I

Funny name, Chyron, this company that summarizes screens
for us, encapsulating chaotic times in phrases as well as lifting
words of praise and joy as if we're reading liner notes about the lives
around us.
Chyron, perhaps from Chiron, centaur, wise teacher, healer?
How much would reading summaries of what I'd lived,
as if my life were telecast,
teach me about myself, what kinds of wisdom gained from short-
hand understanding?
HIDE   CRAWLING   LETTERS,   LIVE   THE
WORDS   INSTEAD

II

That shortbread we had bought in Grasmere
butter rich, tinned storage saving it for later,
reminding us of awkward paddling in the lake
near Wordsworth's home, the flavor of that day
remembered in each later bite, each glorious rich
reflection of the buttery sun helping
us forget the sunburns and the staleness
SAVOR   THE   SUN   AND   SHORTBREAD

III

Always, the first day of anything, so hard to slow down
the busy-ness, the hurried-ness, the jumpy-ness

of life, but now, it's Day One of Meditation Class, the thrumming
phrases hover: to be a beginner to be more of a beginner
to be only a beginner.
WE   ARE   ALWAYS   BEGINNERS   AT   LIFE

IV

Would we want to read ours daily,
captions making moments clearer,
decoding the disturbing ones, our
personal headlines crawling across our screens,
simplifying the difficult,
organizing the messy, reminding us of all we live, the good
and difficult,
decluttering flotsam of failed conversations
and jetsam of jagged intersections,
gathering in the momentous and the miniscule.
REMEMBER   THIS   MOMENT   AND
LIVE   MOMENTS
WITHOUT   PAUSE,   WITHOUT
NEEDING   ANYTHING
              E   L   S   E

2021

Some final words ~when silence gives way to sound~

Some days I feel most creative when I'm not writing, but thinking about what I want to write about, letting everything that my eyes gaze upon become beautiful possibilities for *soundscapes* that might appear days or weeks or months later—as poetry. My process recoils from a "poem-in-a-box" definition; I rather think my "how" as a writer is best described by the many small journals, notepads, personal folders on my computer, filled with comments like this one from February 2017:

> *A new year—new writings new/old me—entry for today is 'lose control'*
> *per Natalie Goldberg, and yet, for me, much of my life, I believe, has*
> *been without control—no sense of direction unless someone else was*
> *giving it to me, and me with a pseudo-sense of a path. New year, new*
> *directions—we'll see!*

And then, I take off—the censor gone, the paths open before me, not trying too hard to find the right metaphor or analogy, but feeling my way towards a true center. I keep a finger labyrinth on my desk, reminding me of the many paths that thinking, often followed by writing, will take me—reminding me not to worry about the center as the beginning, but to feel the gentle boundaries of the many paths that lead not to emptiness, but to other ways in.

Perhaps it is the reminder that what possesses me is what I will write about. The memories that enfold me and mystify me. The stories that were never uttered to me, but hinted at. The moments hidden from me to protect me, ultimately binding me—this is what writing frees. Relationships that hurt rather than healed gave rise to words that could begin the mending. The loneliness that battens and lines my life celebrates solitude and doesn't fear it: the writer's moments as pre-writing give way to whispering, then writing, and, maybe, illumination.

Finitude, which becomes more poignant as I age, is an easier companion than I had imagined because of my writing. My words have become agents for eternity. It's all in the thinking, the taking of a turn of phrase: who might be the voice-over for my life, what is a 'sketch artist', why did my dream last night take me in high heels down a climbing wall?

Finally, it's the sitting, the introspection of self, the awareness of all who will accompany me when I begin to write—whether they are physically present or not—that taps into the desert and the ocean—that forms the piece. The statement. The utterance that will not disturb even if born of distress. The soul's appearance as poem.

Acknowledgements

With gratitude for all the mentors who have touched my life: my teachers at Waltham High School; my professors at Wellesley College; the dear poet Elliot Coleman at Johns Hopkins in The Writing Seminars program; the faculty at Santa Clara University helping me hone my teaching and counseling skills; my students from high schools and colleges sharing the richness of many conversations; my writing workshop friends, especially from Writing it Real with mentor/guide Sheila Bender; my Gifts of the Spirit writing group with LeMel and Eileen; the literary magazine editors who have said 'yes' to me, and those who've said 'no' with great encouragement; and the clergy who have asked me to share my poetic voice in many ways, helping me find the sacred in the ordinary over and over again.

With love for my family, my dear ones, especially my sons Jimmy and Brad, who have been with me through so much of my life.

With tenderness for my granddaughter Polina and my daughter-in-law Maryna, and, especially, for Jim Bathgate who has helped me understand how patience manifests itself as love.

With loving memory of my mother Dorothy, who taught me to love words, to write words lovingly, and to share my stories, as I lived them, stored as poems, literary memories that continue to last.

Author's Biographical Notes

Barbara Simmons grew up in Boston and now resides in
California—the coasts inform her poetry. A graduate of Wellesley
College, she received an MA in the Writing Seminars from Johns
Hopkins, mentored by poet Elliot Coleman, and an MA in
Educational Administration from Santa Clara University. A retired
educator, teacher and counselor, she savors the smaller parts of
life and language, exploring words as ways to remember, envision,
celebrate, mourn, and understand. Her publications have included
*Santa Clara Review, Hartskill Review, Boston Accent, NewVerse News,
Soul-Lit, 300 Days of Sun, Capsule Stories, Isolation Edition, Capsule
Stories, Autumn 2020, and Capsule Stories, Winter 2020, Writing it
Real,* and the *Journal of Expressive Writing.*

Printed in Canada